WHEN THE HONEYMOON'S OVER

When the Honeymoon's Over

Building a Real-Life Marriage

Kathy Collard Miller & D. Larry Miller

Harold Shaw Publishers
Wheaton, Illinois

The authors thank Charles M. Sell for his kind permission to use the exercise on pp. 140-141.

Edited by Robert Bittner and Elizabeth Cody Newenhuyse

Cover and interior design by David LaPlaca

ISBN 0-87788-565-6

Library of Congress Cataloging-in-Publication Data

Miller, Kathy C. (Kathy Collard), 1949-
    When the honeymoon's over— : building a real-life marriage / Kathy
Collard Miller and D. Larry Miller.
        p.   cm.
    ISBN 0-87788-565-6
    1. Marriage–United States. 2. Married couples—United States—Psychology.
3. Man-woman relationships—United States. I. Miller, D. Larry. II. Title.
    HQ536.M54 1997
    646.7'8—dc21   97-10278
                                                            CIP

02 01 00 99 98 97

10 9 8 7 6 5 4 3 2 1

Contents

was New Year's Eve, 1966. I really enjoyed being with Kathy. She was bright and attractive. I took her to my church where she accepted the Lord and then grew strong in him. As we grew closer to each other and to God, we became confident God wanted us to be husband and wife.

And now we almost are!

Larry grins back at me as I float down the aisle toward him, my prince. Our marriage will be perfect. We know God is leading our relationship.

After repeating our memorized vows and being pronounced man and wife at exactly 7:21 P.M. (Joyce, our thoughtful bridesmaid, remembers to look at her watch), we hurry back down the aisle, beaming our joy to finally be one flesh. Life has just begun!

But just a few months later, things don't seem quite so perfect. Little warning signals are beginning to flash. Larry works until 2:00 A.M. on Saturday nights, and I can't wake him up to go to church.

"Larry," I almost shout into his ear as I shake his shoulder. "It's time to get ready for church!"

But I drive off to church alone again, completely disgusted that Larry doesn't think church is important enough to make every effort to attend. A tiny rust spot has begun to form on my prince's armor. *But that's all right,* I reason. *I'm sure I'll be able to buy some Rust Away Foam to make it go away.*

Later at lunch, I coldly answer his questions, trying to make him know I'm ignoring him without appearing to ignore him. Why doesn't he notice I'm upset?

As the months pass, the rust spot grows a little bigger. *A baby will draw us closer together,* I think. *He won't be able to resist a little one.*

Kathy and I are both working, and it's great having the extra money. She says she's unhappy and wants to have children. I would much rather spend the money on my flying hobby. I want her to be happy, though, so we make plans to start a family.

"But, Kathy," I gently warn her, "this really isn't my first priority. You understand that, don't you?"

She nods as her eyes light up with delight, and I'm confident she realizes she'll be responsible for the home and children. I will secure our financial future. I don't want anything to stifle my success.

After Darcy is born and Kathy quits work, I start working a second job in real estate. A few sacrifices now are a small price to pay for future rewards.

By the time we've been married seven years and Mark has also been added to our family, Larry is rarely home. The very character qualities I'd once appreciated in him are now sources of irritation. Why did I ever think his ambition and opinionated attitudes were charming?

One morning Larry announces he's flying to San Jose for the day. I quickly suggest, "Larry, I'll get the kids ready and we'll go with you—"

Larry interrupts me. "Kathy, I'm sorry you can't go because I only rented a two-seater plane. I've already asked Joe to go."

"But, Larry, we never see you. Can't you stay home just this once?"

"Now, Kathy." Larry's voice drops into his patronizing tone. "I've already explained that I'm working all these hours to secure our financial future."

My face grows hot with frustration. "Money isn't helping me cope with these kids. Darcy makes me so angry sometimes."

"That's just typical motherhood blues," he replies, a little too casually. "You'll be fine. I'll be home at ten tonight. You stay home and have a nice, quiet day with the kids."

Larry walks away down the hall, through the laundry room and into the garage, closing the door behind him. It's as if he slammed it in my face. Anger boils within me. "Why can't you be my Prince Charming who meets all my needs?" I mentally scream.

I had been eating an apple, and suddenly my hand is hurling it at the door. The apple shatters, spraying pieces across the ceiling and the walls of the laundry room.

I turn and march into my bedroom, where I drop to my knees beside my bed. "Lord, make that plane crash! I don't care if he ever comes home again."

 As I spend more time away from home, Kathy constantly complains. I just tune her out. I can never please her anyway. If I try to fulfill her requests, she's never satisfied.

"Kathy, I have problems and stresses every day, just like you," I tell her one day. "But I never ask for help. You should just get control."

Kathy's face turns red. "You are so insensitive!"

Turning my attention back to the football game, I think, *She sure is getting angry more often.* Kathy doesn't act like the same bright, energetic girl I married. I'm a night owl, and I would love to have Kathy stay up late with me. But she says the kids make her too tired.

I guess I'm stuck. Even though Kathy seems neurotic,

I must stay committed to this marriage. Divorce is out of the question, but I wonder, *Is this going to be a life sentence?*

 In spite of this hopeless situation, God began a multifaceted process of growth and understanding in our lives. He brought restoration and an incredible joy back into our marriage. He can do the same for you, too.

We want to share with you principles that will strengthen your marriage and bring greater joy and understanding to your relationship. So read on and find out how you can successfully deal with the inevitable rusty spots in your Prince Charming's armor (or the fraying patches in your Lady's velvet gown).

Chapter 2

Different, Not Wrong: Temperaments and Your Marriage

As we began the journey of healing in our marriage, one of the first places God led us was to explore the role of temperament. I found a book by Tim LaHaye entitled *Understanding the Male Temperament.* I was attracted to it because I knew I didn't understand Larry. As I studied the topic, I identified Larry's temperament and pinpointed my own. I realized he and I saw life differently, and that was okay. Before, *different* had always meant "wrong" to me. Now I saw that it might be possible for us both to be right, even though we disagreed.

As Kathy began incorporating these ideas into her interactions with me, her expectations didn't seem as unrealistic. Before, I had wanted to stay away because

something!' I see the big picture and love to delegate to others.

"I'm a natural leader and, even though others don't always admit it, I'm usually right. I really am!

"I remember a time in high school when a new group of friends shook up my world. These new friends were on the swim team and got good grades. I was overweight and got mediocre grades. I was out of my comfort zone and not in control. I immediately began working out and lost weight. I also started studying and excelled without any help. Asking for help meant not being in control and that was too threatening. I achieved my new goals, and life was back as it should be.

"Speaking of my goals: that's my big problem. As a Driver, I wage an ongoing spiritual battle with self-sufficiency. Drivers are the most emotionally under-developed of all the temperaments. Usually we don't even acknowledge we have feelings. But when we be-come aware of them, we think we're losing control, and that's unacceptable. To cover up our emotions, Drivers tend to be impatient, bossy, and inflexible. We demand a lot from others and don't handle their mistakes well. But just think: We get things done!"

Mr. Driver smiles at the audience, hoping to control their reaction toward him. Then he salutes them and walks away with a jaunty step.

The Analytical Temperament

After a few moments, a woman rushes onto the stage, smoothing her skirt with one hand and pushing a stray hair back into place with the other. "I just wanted to look in the mirror one more time," she says to the stage manager. She stops abruptly when she notices the audience. "Oh . . . oh, hi. I'm Ms. Analytical.

"In case you haven't noticed, I want my life and the things around me to be perfect. At the age of thirteen, on New Year's Eve at the stroke of midnight, I took a symbolic bubble bath that cleansed me from all the sins of the previous year. And I vowed that I would never sin in the coming year.

"I reasoned that attaining perfection would make me acceptable and loved by God and other people. But I didn't identify myself as a perfectionist because I could allow some areas in my life to be imperfect. I thought I needed to have every area to be perfect in order to label myself a perfectionist. Now I know that's not true—I *am* a perfectionist.

"As an Analytical, I'm very introspective and constantly analyze my progress. I love facts and details. What I don't love is taking risks or being assertive. I also have a hard time making quick decisions. I work best alone and appreciate accuracy. At my classical Analytical best, my vocabulary includes sentences like 'Let's evaluate' and 'Don't make hasty decisions.' I crave order and to be understood by others. Because I look at life so seriously, it's hard for me to see or use humor.

"One sunny afternoon when I was in the third grade, my best friend, Irene, did something that angered me. I lashed out and punched her right in the nose. I was humiliated and shocked. I reasoned I must never get angry again. I became an expert at repressing my unpleasant feelings—another way of trying to become perfect.

"Yet with these weaknesses, Analyticals have many strengths. We can be talented and artistic, dependable and loyal. We keep things orderly and neat."

Ms. Analytical looks over at the stage manager and asks, "Did I do all right?" He must have nodded, for she smiles, brushes a piece of lint from her blouse, and exits.

The Amiable Temperament

Three minutes pass, and the audience begins to grow restless. Then a man casually meanders onstage, seemingly unaware of being late. He smiles wide at the audience and begins. "Hello, there. I'm Mr. Amiable. I'm a pretty easy guy to get along with. If you don't agree with my opinion, that's okay. I'll just switch and agree with yours.

"Social situations terrify me. When I walk into a room full of people, I feel very uncomfortable, afraid someone won't like me, or I'll say something that someone won't like, and that might lead to a confrontation. I hate confrontations.

"I'm often slow to make decisions because I don't want to rock the boat. If you're around me very long you'll hear me say, 'Whatever you think' or 'Whatever's easiest.'

"I'm a peace-at-any-price kind of guy. If our pastor tells our Bible study group that Matthew follows Luke in the New Testament, and my Driver wife jumps up to argue with him, I'll tell her that maybe our pastor has a newer Bible than ours. Anything to avoid a hassle. That way, everybody likes me.

"I will say, though, that my attitude has caused problems at work. Just recently, I felt someone had not treated my company fairly. When that individual confronted me about my dissatisfaction with their treatment, it was easier for me to try to smooth everything over. I get so angry with myself at times like that, yet my insides just churn like a riverboat paddle whether I know I'm right or not.

"It also concerns me that I could present the wrong kind of image to a lot of people, particularly my children. I don't want them to think people, sometimes even my wife, take advantage of me. Most people don't understand that I just like to leave the job of decision making to others. Usually it's because most of the time it really doesn't matter to me.

"I can easily overlook my strengths . . . like being a sound negotiator. Not long ago, I was asked to help another company during a difficult time. By the time my assignment ended, the man who had been my biggest adversary became my biggest supporter.

"As an Amiable, I'll do what's expected of me, but, particularly at home, I won't do any more than is actually necessary. That's because I always unconsciously ask, 'How much energy will this take?' I guess that's why an Amiable can easily be called lazy. It's fine if you call it that. I just prefer to call it being peaceful and calm."

Mr. Amiable laughs along with the audience and obviously is pleased with the result. After a slight wave of his hand, he strolls off the stage.

There you have the four temperaments—and a varied bunch they are! Here's a look at the basic traits of each:

Expressive

Friendly and talkative	Exaggerates
Good sense of humor	Undisciplined
Creative and charming	Easily distracted
Energetic and restless	Loves approval, attention, and
Thrives on compliments	applause

Driver

Dynamic leader	Determined to succeed
Unemotional	Likes opposition
Domineering and independent	Quick thinker
Sees big picture	Lacks empathy
	Intolerant

Analytical

Conscientious	Loves details
Perfectionistic	Good listener and loyal friend
Loves to think	Compassionate
Appreciates culture and the arts	Easily depressed
Thorough and organized	Remembers hurts/easily resentful
	Unrealistic expectations

Amiable

Easygoing and calm	More a watcher than a doer
Quick-witted	Low energy level
Low awareness of own emotions	Worrier
Excellent mediator	Lacks self-motivation
Capable	Easily judges others
Compassionate, listens patiently	Loves to tease

Although not one of us is purely one temperament, we each tend to operate in our temperament's strengths and weaknesses most of the time—especially when we're under stress. When life is going smoothly, it's easier to operate in the strengths of another temperament. (That's called "versatility," a concept we'll explore shortly.) But when we are bombarded by difficulty, we easily slip back into our temperament's reactions, which may not be the healthiest way to deal with adversity.

And, of course, no one temperament is perfect or more desirable than another. Each has its strengths and weaknesses.

 In the past, I thought changing my temperament would take away my problems. Once I understood the temperaments, I could begin to appreciate the way God made me as an Analytical. It was fine for me to enjoy order and routine. With the Holy Spirit's power I could learn to be flexible and lower my unrealistic expectations. Also, as a writer and speaker, I've learned to use humor as I write and give presentations, something that is not naturally my strength.

As a Driver, I have grown to appreciate the truth of Psalm 139:13-16: "For you created my inmost being; you knit me together in my mother's womb. I praise you because I am fearfully and wonderfully made; your works are wonderful, I know that full well. My frame was not hidden from you when I was made in the secret place. When I was woven together in the depths of the earth, your eyes saw my unformed body. All the days ordained for me were written in your book before one of them came to be."

Versatility

After hearing about the temperaments, some people might say to their spouse, "Now you know why I act the way I do, and you'll just have to accept it. I can't change." But the truth is we can utilize the strengths of a different temperament as directed by the Holy Spirit. This is called "versatility."

For instance, even though the Expressive isn't naturally neat and orderly, he or she can use organizational techniques. The Amiable can choose to confront when necessary, and the Driver can learn to be sensitive and compassionate. The Analytical can become flexible and even learn to appreciate spontaneity.

Jesus manifested all the strengths and none of the weaknesses of each temperament. He was "versatile"; he responded to people with the strength of the appropriate temperament in each situation. With the Pharisees, he reacted like an in-charge Driver. With penitent sinners, he responded as a sympathetic Analytical. With the disciples, he had the patience of an Amiable. With children, he was an outgoing and fun Expressive.

Our goal as Christians is to act and react more like Jesus, through the power of the Holy Spirit, with the strengths of an appropriate temperament. In addition, we can learn not to habitually respond toward life out of the weaknesses of our own temperament.

In his book *How to Bring Out the Best in Your Spouse,* author Gary Oliver observes, "Having a mature, healthy relationship not only involves being able to see things from our own perspective, but also being able to see through the eyes of others. Someone once said, 'If the only tool you have in your tool chest is a hammer, you will tend to see every problem as a nail.' If the only language you speak is your own, if you're only able to see things from your point of view, if your way almost always seems like the 'right' way, then you're in for some difficult times." The more versatile we are, the more we'll avoid those "difficult times."

Opposites Attract

There are some natural opposites within the temperaments, and often these opposing personalities end up married to each other.

The Expressive is the other side of the coin of the Analytical. The Expressive's desire for fun balances the Analytical's serious nature. The Amiable is the contrast to the Driver, since the Driver wants to control everything and the Amiable is willing to let her or him do so.

Similarly, each temperament is weak where the opposing temperament is strong. The Expressive helps the Analytical to enjoy life more, and the Analytical helps the Expressive be more down to earth. The Driver influences the Amiable to be more assertive, while the Amiable teaches the Driver to be more easygoing.

Obviously, Drivers don't always marry Amiables; Expressives don't always get together with Analyticals. But even when two Analyticals marry each other, they influence and change each other. It's up to us to see this as a benefit.

 Even though I'm an Analytical, I'm grateful for Larry's Driver nature. It has helped me be more assertive and less overly sensitive.

 And even though I'm a Driver, I've become more compassionate and sensitive because of the influence of Kathy's temperament.

 Now we can thank God for our individual temperaments. As you learn more from this book, we're confident you will also.

Chapter 3

Why Women Love the Trip and Men Love the Arrival

Our first vacation since our honeymoon! I was going to be with my beloved for three days, and I was looking forward to the five-hour drive on our first day. Without interruptions, we could talk and talk. But Larry seemed strangely silent or else gave me one-word replies. *I guess Larry must be intent on driving, so I'll enjoy the scenery,* I thought.

Several hours later, hunger nagged at me. "Aren't we going to stop to eat?" I asked. Larry replied, "I thought we'd just eat the snacks you brought. That way we can get there sooner."

I couldn't believe what I was hearing. "Larry, vacations are times to relax and enjoy your way as you go along."

"Honey, I want to get there before dark," I responded. "Just pull out the chips, okay?" I turned my attention back to the road and immediately got lost in thought. I just loved driving my new sports car (even if it was "new" only to me). It just didn't get better than this.

Something inside me died as my dreams and expectations of a leisurely drive with lots of conversation evaporated. I concluded that Larry didn't like being with me, and I swallowed back tears. *Why does this happen so much?* I agonized. *Why am I constantly being disappointed and finding my opinions ignored?*

Hours later we arrived at our destination but stayed for only two hours. Then it was off to Larry's next scheduled driving goal. When we finally did stop at midnight to sleep, he insisted we get up at 5 A.M. to continue our trek. I had no idea our vacation would be one driving marathon!

I couldn't wait to get back in the car. I'd reached the first goal; now it was time to conquer the next one, just 290 miles away. The driving and arriving was the vacation I really enjoyed.

We laugh now about that first vacation. We had no idea we were facing only the first of many experiences that would show us the contrasts between men and women—to say nothing of the differences caused by our individual temperaments.

In his book *The Joy of Committed Love,* Gary Smalley writes, "I would venture to say that most marital difficulties center around one fact—men and women are TOTALLY different. The differences (emotional, mental, and physical) are so extreme that without a *concentrated effort* to understand them, it is nearly impossible to have a happy marriage."

Smalley goes on to say, "Watch what happens during many family vacations. He is challenged by the goal of driving 400 miles a day, while she wants to stop now and then to drink coffee and relax and relate. He thinks that's a waste of time because it would interfere with his goal."

Evidently Gary Smalley had heard about our first vacation!

Generalities about Gender

Here are some generalities about gender differences. Of course not every observation is going to apply to every person or every marriage, but these are tendencies that need to be taken into account as we relate to our spouses. As you go through this material, try to understand your mate with the goal of not taking everything personally or as a critique of you as a spouse.

Women value relationships; men value objects and concepts. Women tend to be people oriented, whereas men tend to be object- and intellectual-concept oriented. Women react out of their desire to attain security through people; men react out of their desire to attain significance through conquering things and achieving success. Think of most gatherings you go to. The women, most often, cluster together talking about people. The men usually talk to each other about sports or work.

Women like the process; men like the goal. Women love the trip; men love the arrival.

I demonstrated this point on our trip. Kathy looked forward to the time she could have with me, expecting it to bring us closer together. But I just couldn't wait to get there and reach my goal!

Women want to discuss, plan, and get all the details before making a decision. Men usually make quick decisions. A wife may want to sit down with her husband and have a conference about the decision they must make. She sees it as an opportunity to deepen their relationship.

On the other hand, we men usually want to make the decision yesterday. We don't want to make a big deal out of it. Just decide! Get to the goal of decision making. That means we often will act more impulsively. For example, when it comes to spending money, women often get a bad rap, but men clearly are the ones who will spend the big dollars for a new car, boat, or RV— often at a moment's notice. Once again we bagged our prey and parked it proudly in the driveway for all to see.

This difference can be influenced by the temperaments, though. A Driver wife may seem to have this "male" characteristic because she loves to make fast decisions. But generally speaking, women enjoy the process of decision making, and men want it over with.

A month before our wedding, we needed to find an apartment. On our scheduled "apartment shopping day," I envisioned a day of closeness, traveling to several apartment buildings to gather information, going out to lunch, more looking, and finally making the big decision over a romantic dinner that evening. After looking at the first apartment, I found Larry walking toward the manager's office ready to sign on the dotted line. My image of a romantic day was gone!

Because I hadn't shared my vision, Larry had no idea his quick decision pricked a hole in my balloon of expectations. I assumed Larry looked at our day the same way I did.

 I merely saw this decision as something that needed to be done—and the faster, the better. Why make a big deal out of it?

With Kathy's influence, I have learned to value relationship-building opportunities more. This especially applies to sex, most likely the area in this category in which men and women are the furthest apart. Women love the foreplay that precedes sexual intercourse. Men want to just get to the important stuff: orgasm! Now I can appreciate the value of foreplay and can bask in the "afterglow." I realize that touching and talking sparks sexual desire within Kathy. As a result, she is more responsive to me and I feel more successful. (We'll be talking about sex in greater detail in a later chapter.)

 Here's an example of a conversation that shows how differently men and women think:

She (as they drive by a furniture store): "I sure would like to get new living-room furniture."

He: "But we just moved into our new house. We can't afford it yet."

She: "Yeah, but wouldn't it be great to have it?"

He: "Even if we bought it on our credit card, the current high interest rates would really cut into my income. We'll talk about it after I get my raise in July."

She (suddenly turning to him in frustration): "You always squelch my good ideas!"

What was she really looking for? Someone to dream along with her about the details, because women love to think out loud. She wasn't saying she had to have the new furniture right now, just that it sounded like a good idea. She wanted her husband to say, "Yeah, new furniture sure would be wonderful, wouldn't it? I can understand how great that would make our new living room look."

The male mind, however, is terrified that if he gives her such a reply, she'll grab the steering wheel, drive the car into the furniture store parking lot, and immediately spend thousands of dollars on furniture. He can fight that impulse by still telling her they can't afford it—but, along with the cold facts, warm her by giving her the chance to share the emotional details.

Women want intimacy; men want independence. Every human being desires both intimacy and independence, but women tend to favor intimacy over independence, and men tend to favor independence over intimacy.

Women can interrupt someone's conversation but think of it in terms of acceptable "overlapping." Men regard it as rude. This is difficult for women to understand. When women talk among themselves, they will break into the conversation and no one minds. Women consider "overlapping" a way to show their involvement in the conversation, to develop closeness. Men view it as disrespectful because they wait their turn.

In her book, *You Just Don't Understand*, linguistics professor Deborah Tannen explains, "In many of the comments I heard from people I interviewed, men felt interrupted by women who overlapped with words of agreement and support and anticipation of how their sentences and thoughts would end. If a woman supported a man's story by elaborating on a point different from the one he had intended, he felt his right to tell his own story was being violated. He interpreted the intrusion as a struggle for control of the conversation."

This is difficult for women to understand. When women talk, they'll break into one another's conversations and no one seems to mind. Men don't understand this. (Although Professor Tannen did find that men feel comfortable interrupting a woman!)

 Since learning of this concept, I have been observing the reactions of men as I purposely "overlapped" the conversation with them. More often than not, they stopped talking and looked or sounded irritated.

Women want to be helpful; men want to be protective.
Have you ever had a conversation like this with your spouse?

She: "What time do you want to leave for the church social?"

He: "Don't worry, you have time to cook the casserole."
Or:

He: "How many people are coming for dinner tonight?"

She: "You have to be ready to barbecue at 6:30."

If you've had an interaction with your spouse like that, you most likely got frustrated thinking, "Why didn't he (or she) answer my question?" In the first example about the church social, the husband is giving his answer because he wants to protect his wife. The problem is that the wife may take his answer as meaning he's withholding information and trying to be the one in control.

Although the second example is similar to the first in addressing the question, the motivation is different. The wife wants to be helpful by answering what she thinks her husband is really wondering about. She believes she is anticipating her husband's desires and concerns.

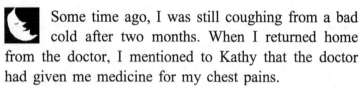 Some time ago, I was still coughing from a bad cold after two months. When I returned home from the doctor, I mentioned to Kathy that the doctor had given me medicine for my chest pains.

"What chest pains?" Kathy exclaimed, concerned and frightened.

I had purposely withheld details of my chest pains from Kathy. I sheepishly replied, "I didn't want to frighten you, so I didn't tell you. For the last week, I've been experiencing chest pains."

"You didn't want to frighten me?" Kathy's voice raised. "I thought you understood that not telling me what's going on weakens my trust in you."

Kathy didn't say it, but she would have liked to "mother" me: be concerned about the problem and make me feel cared for. She wanted to be helpful. It was exactly what I wanted to avoid. I wanted to "protect" Kathy from worry and concern. Now I realize I subconsciously wanted to maintain control. (As it turned out, the doctor ran an EKG and couldn't find anything wrong, concluding I most likely strained a chest muscle from coughing.)

Then I put myself in Kathy's shoes and imagined her making the same choice I had. When I mulled over being cut out of the information loop, I felt uncomfortable. I realized I had inadvertently hurt Kathy by trying to protect her. Trust and honesty are inseparable. You can't have one without the other.

The Keys to Understanding

As we consider these different perspectives of life, ⸺
are the keys to understanding:

1. Acknowledge the differences.
2. Choose to thank God for them, even if you don't feel grateful.
3. See the advantages of looking at life differently.
4. Use the differences to complete and make whole your own perspective.

Proverbs 27:17 tells us that as iron sharpens iron, so one person sharpens another. What area is a struggle for you and your spouse? Are you willing to recognize that God is using it to "sharpen" you; that is, to make you better? Are you looking at your mate's ideas with disdain when her or his perspective is possibly valuable?

Relax and agree with the God who says, "He who heeds discipline shows the way to life, but whoever ignores correction leads others astray" (Prov. 10:17). God may indeed be instructing you through your spouse's gender perspective.

Chapter 4

Assumers and Mind Readers

Two years into our marriage, Larry and I shopped for a new dining-room table. He expressed a desire for a "distressed wood" table, one where tiny pieces were gouged out to make it look old. That was fine with me. In fact, I pictured our children someday sitting at the table doing their homework, and I shared my warm image with Larry.

"Kathy," he said. "Our children can't use this kind of a table."

I stood stunned at his words. How dare he think that his precious table is more important than our children! I quickly thought of several times Larry had made similar choices that indicated his wrong priorities. *He can just pick out any old table he wants, and I'll make sure our children stay away from it!*

 I glanced over at Kathy as I started to point to an oak table with a distressed top, then paused.

She had a look on her face that I couldn't decipher, but it wasn't happy. "Kathy, here's the table I . . . What's wrong?"

"Oh, nothing," she said as she looked away. "Go ahead and get any table you want. I don't really care." Her voice dripped venom.

"Honey, what's wrong?"

When Kathy didn't answer, I shrugged my shoulders. Well, if she wouldn't share with me, I wouldn't pry.

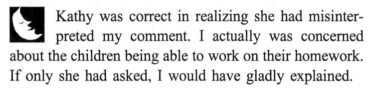 Many years later (seven seems to stick in my mind, but I hope that's not true), I again reflected on that incident as I had many times before. It had become a well-worn illustration to me of Larry's insensitivity to my needs and our children's needs.

Thinking through all this, as the good Analytical that I am, a completely foreign idea unexpectedly surfaced. Could Larry have meant that our children couldn't use the table because the pitted surface of the wood would hinder their ability to write?

Kathy was correct in realizing she had misinterpreted my comment. I actually was concerned about the children being able to work on their homework. If only she had asked, I would have gladly explained.

Our Unspoken Assumptions

The above is only one example of the many assumptions husbands and wives make about each other. Here are some others.

What's important to me should be important to my spouse. Amiable Todd and Expressive Carrie have been married almost sixteen years, and this is an area of struggle for them. She works the day shift; he works afternoons and evenings. This past summer, Carrie asked Todd to take Kaitlyn, their adolescent daughter, to the dermatologist to check on her acne. Carrie hadn't wanted Kaitlyn to miss classes during the school year, but she didn't explain that to Todd.

Todd put it off and soon the new school year started. "I forgot about it," he admitted. "It's no big deal."

"But it is a big deal," Carrie replied. "Kaitlyn will miss several classes because she's in junior high now. It's more difficult to follow through on missed assignments."

"Well, you didn't explain it to me that way," Todd countered.

"I want you to think about things," Carrie persisted. "I shouldn't have to explain everything. It's *obvious* it was better if Kaitlyn went during the summer."

Todd shrugged his shoulders. "I don't want to think."

Todd was not being flippant. As an Amiable who evaluates everything on the basis of "How much energy will this take?" he can quickly relegate something to the "it's not that important to do it now" column of his mind. Besides, it's *not* obvious.

"You mean that if I'd explained the importance of Kaitlyn's appointment during the summer, you would have done it then?"

Todd grinned his Amiable grin that said, "No promises." "But," he quickly explained, "it would have been more likely than not, knowing the reasons why."

Todd and Carrie are improving at casting aside the assumption that "if it's important to me, it should be important to you."

I'll always love that about my spouse. When a couple

is dating, they generally try to put their "best feet forward." Not only that, each tends to view the other in the best possible light. Such positive thinking creates the assumption that the qualities so cherished during courtship—particularly the other person's temperament strengths—will always be valued. But once we're married we begin to say things like the following:

- "Of course I loved our quiet little picnics, but can't we spend a little more money and go to that expensive restaurant for once?"

- "I thought it was exciting that you wanted to go somewhere every night when we were dating, but I'm too tired to keep up with you anymore."

- "I appreciated you being in charge of everything when we were engaged, but I can make some of my own decisions, y'know."

Why is it that the very things we loved in our mates when we were dating can become the kindling wood that sets fire to conflicts today? All too soon, what was once so attractive to us now becomes an irritant. Here are some comments we may say—or hear—if we stop appreciating the strengths of our mate's temperament.

If your mate is an Expressive, you may say: "I loved your enthusiasm and energy for being out with people, but now I'd like to enjoy an evening at home with just us." "I loved talking a lot on our dates, but couldn't we hear what quiet sounds like for once?" "Your tendency to exaggerate seemed fun at the time, but now you're exaggerating my foibles at my expense!"

If your mate is a Driver, you may say: "You may be good at delegating, but I don't want all the responsibility for raising the kids, keeping house, and tending the yard." "Your strong opinions when we were dating made me feel secure, but why can't I ever win an argument?" "It felt good to have someone make quick decisions, but now I'm not even given a chance to think before everything's decided for me."

If your mate is an Analytical, you may say: "Giving me all the psychological reasons for my family's idiosyncrasies was interesting at the time, but I'm tired of getting analyzed." "Your hesitation in making decisions gave me a chance to express myself, but waiting forever for a decision is not my idea of leadership." "Making everything 'just so' seemed like a good trait when we were dating, but requiring perfection in everything I do isn't what I had in mind."

If your mate is an Amiable, you may find yourself saying: "When we were dating, your easygoing attitude seemed so peaceful; now it's just laziness." "Your quick wit was so funny, but now that I'm the brunt of it, it's not so humorous." "You looked at life with such a low-key approach, and I thought I'd never get tired of it. But now I want to have a good, drag-out fight, and you only withdraw."

When we find ourselves making these comments, we assume our spouse changed after we got married. But, says H. Norman Wright in *How to Bring Out the Best in Your Spouse,* our mate hasn't changed—the situation has:

> Most couples enter marriage while they're in the romantic rather than the realistic stage. Maybe this happened to you. Your partner seemed per-

fect, and if there were any noticeable flaws you discounted or ignored them.

Infatuation can color our perception and cause us to overlook even significant differences. You assume the romantic high will continue far into the future.

Since we don't usually think this through consciously or clearly, we may make some assumptions that further nettle our relationship. We can think, *He's doing that on purpose to bother me;* or, *She doesn't love me anymore; otherwise, why would she be trying to make my life miserable?*

Even though we usually don't communicate these thoughts verbally, they flavor the way we react toward our partner. As a result, the unsuspecting spouse perceives a subtle chilling, and thus begins a cycle of misunderstandings and inappropriate reactions. But the cycle can be broken if one partner will communicate this statement, either in words or actions: "I will strive to accept you as you are and not doubt your love. I don't need to assume I know what you're thinking or wanting. Instead, I can ask."

Because we're resisting being defensive, we can keep our voice at a normal tone instead of raising it in anger or hurt. The best chances for healing and clarifying dialogue will then result.

Words mean the same thing to you as they do to me. When you say, "I love you" to your spouse, what do you mean? It may seem ridiculous to ask such a question, but those three words can actually mean a variety of things. They can mean "I like you and the qualities God gave you," or they can mean "I don't feel very loving toward you right now, but I'm trying my hardest to make a decision to love you."

Misinterpretation of even the simplest words can make for amusing mix-ups. My friend Shelly says, "At a local copy shop I recently enlarged some posters that my husband needed for his classroom. The next day he asked me, " 'Where is that copy place?' I told him the directions.

"'No! Where is the place?' he asked me again.

"I started to repeat the directions but he cut me off. 'When I say *where*, I mean what's the name!' "

Shelly's husband seemed to have no comprehension that he wasn't communicating. We speak, and we hear our spouse's words through the filter of our own thinking, woven of the filaments of low self-esteem, insecurity, our temperament, and past traumatic experiences. As the comments of our mate pass through this filter, we interpret those comments based on our own viewpoint. If an Amiable says, "Let's just stay in tonight," an Expressive may hear, "He doesn't want to be seen with me." If a Driver says, "Don't worry about that warning light on the dashboard panel. It won't hurt anything," an Analytical may worry, "He doesn't care about my safety." If that same Analytical suggests, "If you add a little more onion, it'll taste even better," the Driver thinks, *See? I can't do anything to please her.*

Connie and Jared fell into this "language trap" after they'd been married three years. They had met at a pickup basketball game that Connie attended to watch her brother. Jared, therefore, assumed that Connie loved sports. Wrong! Once married, Connie went to few sporting events with Jared. "I didn't want us to live separate lives, but I also didn't want to be bored at all those sporting events," she explains. "Even though I asked him to stay home, he kept going. I was convinced he no longer loved me."

Eventually Connie exploded and personally attacked Jared. He withdrew emotionally and physically, thus reinforcing her belief he didn't care about her. This scenario occurred time after time.

Now listen to Jared's side.

Jared begins, "I was very surprised when Connie didn't go with me to sporting events after we married. She knew how important this was to me. Why was she rejecting something important to me? Maybe she didn't love me as much as before. My natural inclination was to avoid the conflict. I even tried to do loving things for Connie, but they seemed insignificant to her compared to this whole sporting thing. But I just couldn't give it up.

"Every time she told me things like, 'Don't leave me,' I was convinced she was demanding that I stop going to all games. I couldn't risk hearing that."

The tensions between Connie and Jared eventually boiled over into a major fight, but they ended up being able to talk. Jared asked, "What is a reasonable amount of time we should spend together?" His heart was pounding. He was terrified she would say, "Never go to any games."

Connie cocked her head in thought. "Four hours a week of undivided attention."

"That's all?" he asked in surprise.

The more they talked, the more they realized they each had an overblown idea of what the other expected. Even when they used the same words, their definitions weren't the same. He had interpreted her "stay home with me" to mean "never go to another event." Meanwhile, she thought his "I don't want to talk about it" really meant "I'm never going to change so don't bring it up again." In the end, they committed to spending four hours each week focused exclusively on each other. In addition, Connie agreed to attend at least one sporting event each month with a cheerful attitude!

Connie says, "Once I knew I could count on that undivided time with Jared, his absence at sporting events didn't seem so horrible to me. After about a year of attending a sporting event once a month, I actually began to enjoy some sports. Basketball is my favorite."

"Our solution is great," Jared confirms. "Now when I'm gone, I don't feel guilty. I know I'll give Connie my full attention during our dates. And of course I'm thrilled that she's enjoying some sports now."

Don't Assume—Ask!

One of the main goals of this book is to convince you that the person you're married to who at times is driving you crazy has his or her own filter. For the most part, his choices are not intended to make you miserable. He's actually reacting out of his own sense of need and his own goal of making himself feel secure or significant.

What can we do? First, acknowledge your spouse's perspective has value and worth. Second, ask the Holy Spirit to help you understand your mate. Finally, don't assume. Ask until you're fairly confident you understand.

Don't make the same mistakes we did when we went shopping for that dining-room table. We would both act and react differently if we had the opportunity. Now we understand how important it is to ask instead of relying on incorrect assumptions.

Chapter 5

"It's Not My Job"—or Is It?

As I walked to the front door, I noticed the pot with the rosebush sitting on the porch. Larry still hadn't planted it! I went through my typical inner conversation. "If he really loved me, that rosebush would have been planted right away. He's in charge of the yard. It's his job. I don't know how to plant a rosebush and I don't want to learn. If I do, I'll always have to do it, and it should be his responsibility."

Several months later, I realized the bush was dead, its main root coming up through the dirt.

I felt sad and angry. Why hadn't Larry planted my rosebush? *I can't depend on him for anything, not even planting a little bush. Here's more evidence he doesn't really love me,* I thought.

I had no idea that bush was so important to Kathy. As a result, it was easy for me to put it out of my mind. Besides, I didn't know how to plant a rosebush any more than she did. Why was it my responsibility?

Kathy seemed to have such a narrow focus about the chores and responsibilities around our house. I just didn't think of it that way. We didn't have assigned tasks. We should just do whatever was necessary.

I didn't intend to hurt Kathy's feelings, but in my mind, my love for her had nothing to do with planting a rosebush.

I admit now that I could have planted the rose-bush and given up my bitterness. But my low self-esteem continually searched for evidence of Larry's love for me. In addition, my views of men's and women's work prevented me from taking care of it myself.

Although views are changing about what is "man's work" and what is "woman's work," most of us still come into marriage with clear expectations of who will do what.

Reflect on your own attitudes with the help of the following survey. Consider the various aspects of life and marriage, and rank them according to their level of importance for you. Then discuss your answers with your spouse, with the goal of learning more about each other.

	Very Important	Somewhat Important	Not Important
A clean house			
Dinner ready on time			
Gourmet food			
Dressing properly/nicely			
Playing games together			
Spouse disciplining children			
Having a regular date			

	Very Important	Somewhat Important	Not Important
Spouse cooking occasionally			
Planning budget together			
Spouse making most decisions			
Spouse initiating sexual interaction			
Joint checking account			
Yard work			
Sleeping in on weekend			
Exercising regularly			
Keeping diet			
Planning vacations			
Spending time with extended family			
Using leisure time for home projects			
Using leisure time to watch TV			
Spouse baby-sitting children			
Professional does repairs			
Purchases over $30 be decided together			

As you and your spouse take this test, you may find fertile ground for discussion. As you do, take into account a principle developed by Willard Harley, Jr. In his book *Give and Take,* Harley wrote, "Years ago, I created a concept that helped me explain how married couples, once in love, can come to hate each other; how they change from compatibility to incompatibility. I call it the Love Bank. Good experiences deposit 'love units,' leading you to like or even love a person. Bad experiences withdraw units, leading you to dislike or even hate a person."

Expectations of roles within marriage can easily make a withdrawal in that "love bank." Harley also notes, "Domestic responsibilities, never a high priority for most men, usually become a very low priority when they have new families. . . . This can create considerable friction in many homes, especially if the wives also work and therefore experience the same pressures. Unless a couple can act on all this with honesty and intelligence, Love Bank balances are sure to suffer."

Let's look at several aspects of roles in marriage and see what we can learn about preventing withdrawals from our "love bank."

Around the House

Before Eddie and Barbara married, their premarital counselor told them, "Based on your test scores, you shouldn't get married." But they've proven the counselor wrong: fourteen years later, they're still married. Even so, there have been tough times of growing and changing.

Expressive Barbara remembers racing home from work each night to fix elaborate meals. She wanted them to be perfect and ready exactly when Analytical Eddie walked through the door. Then, one night, dinner wasn't ready!

"Oh, Eddie, dinner isn't ready. Please forgive me!"

Eddie looked at her with surprise. "Honey, it's all right."

"But doesn't it make you feel loved when dinner's ready?"

"Barbara, you don't have to do everything perfect in order for me to keep loving you. I love you unconditionally, even if you never have dinner ready."

Barbara explains, "That was a new concept for me, because I had lots of hoops for Eddie to jump through. I believed I could measure his love for me through his actions. For instance, my father washed and filled my mother's car with gas every week. To me, that was my father's demonstration of love for my mother. If he had stopped doing that, I would have concluded that he had stopped loving her. I expected Eddie to do that very same thing for me. When he didn't, I was crushed. A part of me wondered, *How am I going to know he loves me?"*

Many of us grew up with the influence of TV comedies where distinct assignments of household responsibilities were modeled and every conflict was solved in thirty minutes. The modern family is no longer so precisely cut out of solid-color polyester fabric. Often, dads and moms are working full-time, and the children are in school or child care. Even if a mom does stay home and care for the children, there's no reason that Dad can't pitch in and help around the house. More and more husbands feel comfortable doing just that.

We have friends who have found a wonderful mix in the roles they take on. John loves to cook. As a home-based computer worker, he's available for—and loves—his "job" of making dinner every night, something he's done for the twenty-two years of their marriage. His wife, Janet, comes home from her office job and takes on the bill paying and taxes.

Most women would love their husbands to take on more responsibilities around the house, even though they may not expect them to cook every night. Unfortunately, a man's ability to "compartmentalize" his life often gets in the way of seeing what needs to be done.

Harry and Susan struggle with this issue. They've been married ten years and have two sons. Analytical Susan works part-time while the boys are in school but still keeps the house perfect. "When Harry gets home from work, he vegetates in front of the TV or plays computer games," Susan explains. "I try to be sensitive to letting him have time to relax because he's an Amiable, but he walks past unfolded laundry. I can't do that."

Harry is able to "compartmentalize," that is, to focus on one thing and ignore everything else around him. He responds, "Susan, if you would stop feeling responsible for everything, you could relax. Have the boys do the laundry." But perfectionistic Susan envisions towels improperly hung in the bathroom and wrinkled underwear.

How can similar families face the collision of careers, roles, and housework? First, make a list of all the chores your household requires, along with other normal responsibilities such as car repair and servicing, animal care, and so on.

Next, discuss how chore assignments were handled in the family you grew up in. Many times, sharing the expectations formed in your childhood can shatter the idea that your spouse's lack of cooperation is a reflection of their lack of love.

Third, talk about each responsibility and assign tasks based on desire, enjoyment, ability, and time availability. For unclaimed tasks, you might consider paying for professional help. If that's unrealistic, consider taking turns each month at the undesirable tasks. Or do them together as a way of making it more fun.

Fourth, don't let perfectionistic expectations prevent you from appreciating your spouse's efforts. If you think a chore requires perfection, volunteer for it yourself.

Recently, I returned home from a speaking engagement and sighed with relief to find the dinner dishes done. Larry stood nearby with a telltale Cheshire Cat grin that let me know he was proud of his gallant deed. I gave him a kiss of appreciation and a loud "thanks so much." But just then I realized the counter had not been wiped off. Didn't he know the kitchen wasn't clean until the counter was scrubbed? The battle between "doing it right" and being grateful began in my heart. And being grateful won! I didn't even mention the counter. The next evening Larry did the dishes again when I had to rush off to a meeting. Being grateful pays off!

Surprises are so much fun! I found a need and filled it but wasn't aware that my efforts were so lacking. Kathy wisely kept her opinions to herself. If she had been critical or offered on-site instruction on the proper methods of dishwashing, I might have been a little irritated or less motivated to do it the next day.

Early in our marriage it seemed I didn't have too many opportunities to make a significant contribution to chores or duties outside those I naturally assumed, like taking the trash out or making small repairs. Now that Kathy is flying around the country speaking, I find myself with ample opportunities to take a small burden away now and then.

If you've been successful in assigning tasks but the tasks still don't get done, just remember: anger won't get it done either. Let the natural consequences run their course. For instance, if he's assigned to wash a load of whites, when he runs out of T-shirts he'll either go without or run that load fast! And while you're waiting for the whites to be cleaned, remember: taking your spouse's "disobedience" personally won't bring compliance. Usually, he or she isn't being uncooperative to make you angry; his chore just has less value to him than other responsibilities.

Bev and Brian have used humor to relieve the tension. Only married for nine months, Bev laughs as she tells the story of how Brian left his wrench on the floor after fixing the TV. Bev found herself initially getting miffed but decided to see how long it would take Brian to put the wrench away. After three days, she couldn't stand it anymore. She called out excitedly from the living room, "Brian, Brian, come here. You've got to see this. It's amazing!" Brian rushed into the room. Bev was "walking" the wrench across the floor. "Brian, look! The wrench is walking. It wants to go back to the toolbox!"

Brian quickly took the wrench out to the garage, chuckling as he went.

Repairs and Projects

Juleanne laments, "Stephen and I talked about a lot of things before we got married, and we thought we knew each other pretty well. But now that we've been married almost four years, I've decided I didn't ask the most important question: Do you plan to finish do-it-yourself projects?"

Can marital bliss really be found in such circumstances? Here are some guidelines for do-it-yourselfers:

Be grateful. Even if the current project is moving along slowly, praise him or her for the work done in the past.

Create a word picture of success. Say something like, "I just can't wait till our new family room is completed. Won't it be great to sit by the fire and rub your feet?" (Include whatever is valuable to your spouse.)

Reevaluate what is truly "doing it correctly." Priscilla believes a project's tools should be put away at the end of each day. Her loves-to-repair husband, Jerry, leaves tools out so that he can get a fast start the next time. Their compromise? Priscilla allows small items to sit and wait for the next opportunity, but Jerry must put away anything bigger than three feet. They've had some pretty wild and fun times over measuring an item and determining which category a three-feet-one-inch item goes into.

Appreciate the discomfort the project brings to the other person. Jerry is able to abide by the compromise because he understands Priscilla's need for control and orderliness as a Driver. Priscilla, on the other hand, decided that requiring the project area to be totally straightened prevented Jerry, who is an Amiable and has limited energy, from spending time with the family. Each realized adjusting their expectations worked to their own advantage.

Give unconditional cooperation. One time when Jerry left out the three-foot, six-inch sawhorse in the living room, she was tempted to renege on her promise of making her famous cinnamon rolls as a reward for his compliance. Instead, when Jerry came home from work, she popped a warm piece of cinnamon roll in his mouth and said with a smile, "When you put the sawhorse away, you'll get more."

Leisure Time

Sally, an Analytical who works a full-time job, thinks Saturdays are the time to do all the housework. Her husband, Dick, an Amiable, thinks it's the day to watch sports on TV. When Expressive Sam thinks of holidays, he envisions a day of golf. His wife, Sandra, a Driver, plans big family get-togethers. Amiable Candace regards Sunday as the day to do an extended Bible study and take a nap. Her goal oriented Driver husband, Ralph, sees

Sunday as the day to build a new shelf in the den.

Leisure time can become a point of real contention within families, especially when we don't express our expectations. Here are some ideas for doing just that.

1. Talk about your expectations a day or two ahead of the leisure time. Don't assume your mate is thinking the same way you are. For holidays, express your ideas weeks or months ahead, so you have time to plan.
2. Share with a flexible attitude. Relax and ask God to guide you.
3. Try to fit in something for everyone or else compromise with, "I'll be glad to cooperate with your priority this time. Next time you agree to do my idea."
4. Hold the plans loosely in your heart. Circumstances can always change.

Extended Family

Because each of us is affected by our own family of origin, it's hard for us to comprehend living any other way. When we begin dating that special person, our eyes begin to open somewhat to another way of living, but it's as if gauze covers our perception. We can't quite imagine that we'll have to change our lifestyle. So we put up with it, even convincing ourselves that we can fit into these new expectations.

Pastor and author Walter Wangerin, Jr., calls this "idealization." In *As for Me and My House,* he explains:

> Love lies a little. Love, the desire to like and to be liked, feels so good when it is satisfied, that

it never wants to stop. Therefore, love edits the facts in order to continue to feel good. Love allows me an innocent misperception of my fiancée, while it encourages in her a favorable misperception of myself. If it isn't blind, it does squint a bit. Love idealizes both of us. This is natural. It isn't wrong or bad. Listen: marriage is such an intimidating commitment that we need a strong inducement to make it; we all need to be persuaded; and the idealization of the prospective partner is exactly that persuasion.

 We experienced that in the area of Christmas gift giving. When we were dating, Kathy commented during our first Christmas together: "You only have one present?" I didn't think it was odd until I saw the multitude of presents under Kathy's tree. It seemed to me they really overdid it. Years later, as our children Darcy and Mark were growing up, the issue of gift buying brought real conflict. Kathy felt compelled to buy lots of gifts for the children as a way of showing love. My Driver and logical side of thinking believed it to be a waste. One or two gifts for each child was quite sufficient.

 How can couples mediate these differences? First, realize—as we've already discussed—that if your mate comes at things from a different perspective, it doesn't mean he or she is uncaring and insensitive. Second, recognize your spouse isn't deliberately being obstinate; it's just the way he was raised. Although each of you may believe his perspective is correct, acknowledging that "different isn't always wrong" may elicit some tenderness toward the opposing viewpoint. Third, release tension by talking about your own perspective. Fourth, relate how the activity makes you feel. Finally, reconcile the differences by each giving and taking something from the other's position.

 I told Larry, "Buying gifts for the children makes me feel satisfied, as if I'm expressing my love for them." Even so, I learned to buy fewer gifts and realized love isn't measured by the number of presents. I still buy more gifts than Larry prefers, but he recognizes I've brought my quota way down.

 You may be thinking, *Well, that's well and good if you have a spouse who will compromise. I don't. He (or she) won't give in even a little.*

At that point, you're tempted not to give in to anything. But could it be that, by making a small step toward compromise, you might soften your spouse's heart? The Bible encourages that kind of response. When it talks about choices like forgiveness, it never gives a condition like "when they ask for your forgiveness." God can strengthen us to meet our spouse's needs and believe that he will meet ours.

 Understanding that we idealized our relationship before the wedding, and then faced reality after the wedding, can help us cope with expectations now. The husband who promised to help with the chores isn't neglecting them now because of his unhappiness with his wife, but because chores aren't really the most important thing to him.

 Or maybe your wife promised to cheer you on while watching you change the oil in the car. She had every intention of doing that, but now the baby is crying. We don't intentionally disappoint our mates. It's just that preparing for marriage involved idealism; living out the marriage involves realism.

Do your best to accept the other person and relinquish unrealistic expectations. You'll be more content and so will your spouse. And he may even make the effort to wash the dishes without being asked!

Chapter 6

After I Get Him to the Altar, I'll Alter Him

As my disillusionment with Larry deepened, I was always trying to figure out how to make him meet my needs. One day I thought of giving him a surprise birthday party as a way of getting his attention and love. *After all,* I reasoned, *I would love for Larry to give* me *a party. I know I've turned into a nagging wife, so maybe doing something nice for him will turn our marriage around.*

Several weeks later, Larry returned home from a tennis game (the timing had been carefully orchestrated) to a house full of people yelling, "Surprise! Happy birthday!" I'd pulled it off! He was dumbfounded. The look on his face confirmed that he didn't know a thing about all my plans. I was ecstatic. This was sure to work!

But it didn't. Over the next couple of weeks, Larry worked just as many hours. Although he thanked me for the party several times and seemed genuinely pleased, it didn't translate into what I wanted: his attention and affection.

When Kathy threw the party for me, I didn't have a clue what she really wanted from me. I really appreciated the fun time with our friends, but it never occurred to me that Kathy had another agenda. I was angry when I learned of her motives. Her attempt to manipulate me took away the specialness of the event. All the time she was expecting something for herself. My happiness was clearly secondary.

I also was puzzled by Kathy's behavior. At that time I was reasonably content with my life and marriage. Compared to most, it seemed pretty good, even better than many. I never entertained any thoughts about improving or growing our marriage. I figured, good is enough, why strive for more?

Kathy's unhappiness seemed to be her responsibility. After all, we shared the same marriage. I was making choices to enjoy it the best I could. Why couldn't she?

What Is a Marriage For?

Men and women have different views of the purpose of marriage. Often a man gets married because all that dating is draining financially, emotionally, and physically. A woman, on the other hand, sees the wedding as the *beginning* of a continual courtship experience.

When he concentrates on other things after the honeymoon, it's a shock to her. She dejectedly thinks, *I thought he wanted to marry me so that we could be together and nourish each other forever. I expected my Prince Charming to stay at the castle, but instead he's off fighting fire-breathing dragons. So, of course, I have to get him to change his perspective. Since I'm convinced*

God wants him to be a loving husband, I am obligated to help him change.

The groom, however, doesn't see the situation in the same way. To him, his wife is THE ONE. He loves her just the way she is and doesn't want her to change!

H. Norman Wright, in *How to Bring Out the Best in Your Spouse,* writes, "More women than men seem to voice concern over seeing their spouses change. And that seems to be obvious as reflected in the numbers of books written for women on how to understand, figure out, and get along with a man."

This difference in attitude has a lot to do with the fact that God has made women to be interested in relationships, more specifically, making them better at it. In his book *The Joy of Committed Love,* author Gary Smalley notes:

> The woman intuitively has a greater awareness of how to develop a loving relationship. Because of her sensitivity, initially she is usually more considerate of his feelings and is enthusiastic about developing a meaningful, multilevel relationship: that is, a relationship having more facets than just a sexual partnership. She wants to be a lover, a best friend, a fan, a homemaker, and an appreciated partner. The man, on the other hand, does not generally have her intuitive awareness of what the relationship should become. He doesn't have an intuitive awareness of how to encourage and love his wife or how to treat her in a way that meets her deepest needs.

When her husband begins to disappoint her by not fulfilling all her fantasies (known and unknown), the new wife concludes she needs to change him. And that's when trouble starts.

The Myths about Manipulation

At this point, chances are she will find herself buying into the myths about manipulating her husband. And it can work the other way with husbands buying into these beliefs. Either way, these myths can harm a marriage.

If you change, I'll get my needs met. David and Sally have conquered this myth, for the most part. Sally admits, "I was the oldest child in my family, and after my parents' divorce I was in control. I came into marriage looking for someone I could boss. I interpreted love as meaning David would cooperate with my ideas. When he had different ideas about how something should be done, it seemed to spell 'rejection' to me. I felt compelled to argue and try to get my own way."

"When Sally kept trying to make me do everything her way, I finally concluded it wasn't worth the effort of going against her," says David. "I withdrew. In many areas, I let her be boss by saying, 'Fine.'"

"I knew I'd gotten my way, but deep down inside, I didn't like it. Eventually it bothered me so much I asked David, 'Why did you stop talking to me?' He told me that I disagreed with everything he said and it was no longer worth it. I realized he was feeling put down by my constant arguing. I'd never really seen it that way before. Now I'm really trying to consider his opinion just as valid as mine. I'm also correcting my wrong idea that love means he'll do everything I say."

Ultimately, only God can meet any of our needs fully.

He may choose to meet some of our needs thɪ.
mates, but in the long run, only God is a pern.
source of happiness, security, significance, and conteɪ.
ment (Phil. 4:19).

If you change, I can be assured you won't go back to your old habits. Alan and Tina have come a long way since they married thirteen years ago. Because of Alan's drug use and workaholism, Tina felt lonely and isolated. When a neighbor invited her to a Bible study, she accepted Jesus' love into her life. Though she prayed for Alan continually, his addictions grew worse. She saw no alternative other than to divorce him because of his bad influence on their children.

Threatened with losing his family, and challenged by some godly men, Alan also dedicated his life to Christ.

Together, they had begun a wonderful adventure in seeking God. But the fear of Alan's sliding back into his old sin patterns made Tina try to manipulate him to perform as a Christian. "Everything I said was meant to make him stay on the straight and narrow," she says. "If Alan turned on the oldies station in the car, I panicked. I just knew that old music would make him want to start using drugs again. I thought Christians should only listen to Christian music."

Amiable Alan explains, "I only listened to the oldies music when I was with her so that we could have fun together and relax. When I drove by myself, I always listened to praise music and sermon tapes. I couldn't believe Tina was so uptight."

"Now I understand," Tina continues, "that all my manipulative devices were meant to guarantee that Alan wouldn't go back to that old lifestyle and leave me. I

I tell myself over and over again the
y doesn't have to rest on Alan alone.
iusic is fun. Alan's love for God is what
t the kind of music he listens to."

e of Alan and Tina, it really boils down
1 for the growth of your mate. We can't
change a..., e, we can only influence him.

If you change, I'll know you love me. A man's philosophy is "If it ain't broke, don't fix it." Interpretation: "Why do we need to talk about our relationship? It's fine, isn't it?" A woman's philosophy is "Let's make it even better. In fact, if you truly love me, you'll *want* to improve it."

"To many women, the relationship is working as long as they can talk things out," notes linguist Deborah Tannen. "But to many men, the relationship isn't working if they have to continue talking it over."

When a wife says, "Let's talk about our marriage," a man immediately concludes something's wrong and that he's the guilty one! If a woman instead says something like, "There's no big problem; I just enjoy talking about our relationship," she may defuse his fear of being confronted.

But it's not always just the woman who wants improvement. An Analytical male like George can focus on it also. His wife, Charlotte, is an Expressive who finds great difficulty in being organized and efficient. Charlotte says, "When George would get upset with me for not being able to keep a structured routine in our home, I felt like a failure."

"Charlotte didn't seem to try hard enough," George says. "When dinner wouldn't be ready on time, or when the laundry wasn't done, I figured she just didn't love me. I was convinced that knowing how important it was to me would make her be more organized."

After studying the temperaments, George and Charlotte have a better understanding of their weaknesses. George says, "Her Expressiveness makes it difficult to meet my demands, so instead I'm learning to be more realistic." Charlotte replies, "I think I've actually improved more now that I have George's understanding. He realizes I love him even when I fail to meet his needs for an uncluttered house."

If you change, we won't have any problems. This myth is especially prevalent in a marriage where one mate is a Christian and the other is not, or is not growing spiritually. The saved spouse can easily believe, *If he (or she) will come to know Christ, Jesus will change him. I won't have any problems because together we'll be able to take them all to Jesus.*

Pat DeVorss, who has been married to an unbeliever for many years, says, "The problems that bother a saved spouse may not be the result of being married to an unbeliever at all. Every person has flaws whether or not he's a Christian. Even if your mate becomes a Christian, his or her basic temperament and personality will most likely not change that much."

As we've learned, each temperament has strengths and weaknesses. The basic temperament of someone who comes to know Christ will not be altered. She most likely will change to some degree, as we all do, but she won't become perfect.

If you change, I won't feel embarrassed about your

behavior. Martha is almost to the point where she doesn't want her husband, Darren, to attend church with her anymore. Invariably, he falls asleep during the sermon. She usually jabs him in the ribs and hisses, "You're making everyone look at us. Wake up!" Martha thinks her husband is a reflection of her. Her insecurity prevents her from knowing the truth: that her husband is only a reflection of himself.

We've noticed time and time again in working with couples that the trait or weakness that one spouse dislikes in the other is often the very thing others appreciate about that person. You may not value your husband's love for details, yet friends call him to find out his opinion on buying a car because he's read the latest consumer magazines. Maybe you don't appreciate your wife's gift of gab, but she receives invitations to everyone's party because she brings it to life.

You may say, "But everyone is calling Don on the phone and he doesn't have time for me," or "Susie is the life of the party, but she isn't lively around me."

Could it be that your lack of appreciation or criticism of your mate's strength (which you perceive as a weakness) has caused him to seek love and significance from others? He or she has given up trying to get it from you.

That's often the case when we try to manipulate a spouse. We may attempt it through subtle hinting or pouting and moping. Blaming and trying to use guilt often seems appropriate, too. Wives don't enjoy the manipulation tool of nagging, yet they can easily fall prey to it. Proverbs 27:15 warns, "A constant dripping on a day of steady rain and a contentious woman are alike" (NASB).

Another destructive tool is criticism. It seems that pointing out her error or weakness will motivate a spouse

to make changes. Yet, just like negativism, ...
the spouse think, *I can never please him. I* ,
give up.

If those things don't work, it's tempting to ...
something more spiritually minded *should* work. ...
ing the Bible as a weapon to try to convince hi., ne's
wrong won't work either. When I (Kathy) speak on this
topic, I'll often mention that leaving the Bible open on
his pillow, turned to a "convicting" verse, isn't usually
effective. The women laugh because they can relate—
whether their husbands are saved or not!

Motivation, Not Manipulation

We know these negative reactions are inappropriate.
Proverbs 12:4 says, "A worthy wife is her husband's joy
and crown; the other kind corrodes his strength and tears
down everything he does" (TLB).

How can we be "worthy" spouses? Try these techniques.

Distinguish between faults, diversities, and sins.
Faults are behavior patterns we pass along to others
through our example. Diversities are the different perspectives we each bring into marriage and should actually
be appreciated. But sin in our husband or wife should
be confronted. If we mix up those three, we may over-
react or respond inappropriately to a fault or diversity.

**Evaluate how important a particular request for
change really is.** If you're demanding change in many
unimportant areas, your spouse may feel discouraged and
not try at all. If you instead focus on one major tension and
gently encourage change, you'll receive a better response.
Willard Harley, Jr., in his book *Give and Take,* suggests
replacing selfish demands with thoughtful requests. "A

ghtful request begins, *How would you feel about . . .* and then you make your request. This question makes all the difference in the world. For one thing, it reflects consideration of your spouse's feelings, something that a selfish demand blatantly ignores."

Appreciate any steps of growth. As we teach on dealing with perfectionism, we share the "One Percent Principle," the idea that even one percent growth is significant. For perfectionists, one percent doesn't seem valuable, but it is still growth. Be realistic about what your spouse can actually do. Take into account the past trauma or dysfunction that influences him. (For more information on perfectionism, see *When Counting to Ten Isn't Enough*).

Realize that, with time, your mate will change. Change is a basic foundation of life, and, for the most part, people grow better as they mature.

That has happened within our marriage. In many ways, we didn't force the other person to change, we just "rubbed off" on each other. As an insecure and nonassertive Analytical, I have grown more assertive from seeing Larry's Driver strengths.

Because of my Driver temperament, I'm usually an uncompassionate person, but I am now more understanding toward Kathy and others because of Kathy's natural influence.

In *How to Bring Out the Best in Your Spouse,* H. Norman Wright talks about how he realized his wife, Joyce, had changed him:

> Recently my brother and I made a quick overnight trip to my place at Lake Arrowhead so he could

see the new addition we had made to our home. This was one of the few times my wife, Joyce, wasn't with me.

As my brother and I prepared to leave the next morning, I went through a very set routine of cleaning and getting everything in order for several couples who were coming to use the place that weekend. As I left, it struck me that I had just cleaned the house the way Joyce would have! A few years ago I wouldn't have done it that way or even thought of doing it that way. What happened? Joyce taught me. I learned from her. I was doing it her way. I had changed.

You and your spouse are also "rubbing off" on each other without even realizing it. Trying to force someone to change usually only blocks that natural occurrence.

Stimulate change within yourself. Honestly consider how you might be contributing to the tension within your marriage. This will involve a change in the filter through which you view your marriage. Since we're often used to looking through that filter, ask an impartial friend whether she or he sees responses on your part that exacerbate the problem. Allow God to make you a better person by seeing what he's teaching you through your mate. Admitting your own faults, along with asking forgiveness, will soften your spouse's heart more than a judgmental, self-righteous approach.

Proverbs 9:8-9 (NASB) gives us some guidelines for growing in wisdom: "Do not reprove a scoffer, lest he hate you; reprove a wise man, and he will love you. Give instruction to a wise man, and he will be still wiser; teach a righteous man, and he will increase his learning." Are you a scoffer or a wise man? It depends on whether you receive reproof and instruction.

Some people like having lists to follow, others don't. When I was speaking about marriage to an adult Sunday school class, I suggested a wife get everything ready for the chore she wanted done and then invite her husband to join her in doing it. Afterward a man spoke to me saying, "I don't agree with your suggestion. That would make me feel manipulated. I would prefer my wife just make a list and then not nag me. I'll get it done sooner that way."

Find out what techniques motivate your spouse the most and then use them.

Tolerate consequences. Proverbs 19:19 (NASB) says, "A man of great anger shall bear the penalty, for if you rescue him, you will only have to do it again." Most of us not only don't want our mate to suffer the consequences of their poor choices, we don't want to suffer along with them.

Many years ago, we decided Larry should pay the bills so that he would be aware of where the money was going. But Larry didn't enjoy doing it and was gone most of the time anyway. I daily watched the bills stack up unpaid, even though I gently reminded Larry about them.

As the stack got higher, I began to believe Larry had invented a new hobby: collecting bills. When he finally did get around to paying them, there were late charges. I had to cut back my household spending and that made me angry. But soon I saw Larry was "paying" too. He couldn't fly as much when the money had to go for late charges.

Over many months, he got to the bills sooner and sooner, and he learned to enjoy paying them right away. Eventually we bought a computer, and he began tracking all our financial records on it. Then he decided to study to become a certified financial planner and became the only CFP in the United States who was also a policeman. How grateful I was that I hadn't taken the bill-paying job back, even though I had to pay some consequences along with Larry.

Confront appropriately. Here are some guidelines for confronting you may want to follow:

- Pick a good time and place, one with few distractions.

- Have good motives; desire the best for the other person, not his hurt.

- Don't expect a particular response.

- Be willing to forgive.

- Prepare what you'll say: write it out, practice it.

- Be firm, but avoid name-calling or screaming.

- Admit your wrongdoing.

- Stay on the issue; don't exaggerate or threaten.

- Don't use absolute words like: *never, always, all the time, every day, constantly.*

Communicate with "I" messages. "You" messages

make your spouse feel defensive because it sounds as if you're blaming and trying to manipulate. Instead, "I" messages express what you're feeling and thinking without demanding change. Here are some examples:

"You never pay the bills" becomes "I feel stressed when the bills pile up, but I feel peaceful when they're paid. My expectation was that each bill would get paid right away. What was your expectation?"

"When you don't do what I say, I feel that you aren't supporting me" becomes "I feel discouraged when my desires aren't considered important, but I feel cheerful when they are. My expectation was that we would listen and try to please each other. What was your expectation?"

"You're never home" becomes "I feel lonely when I spend so much time by myself, but I'm enthusiastic when we're together. My expectation was that we would spend a lot of time together. What was your expectation?"

"I" messages will not solve all your problems, but they can lay a foundation for good communication and conflict resolution.

Try the A-B communication method. Designate the husband or wife as "A" and the other as "B." A gets to speak for three minutes without being interrupted by B. When the time is over, B must say in his or her own words what A said. Then A can gently state any corrections. Then the roles are reversed, with B addressing the same issue for three minutes and A then repeating what was heard. This technique helps each person feel he or she is really heard and prevents interruptions and arguments.

We've talked throughout this chapter about how our mates cannot meet all our needs. Believing they can—if only we are able to change them—is a dead-end road. Instead, we can try to communicate our needs and then look to God ultimately to make us feel loved and significant. He alone is powerful enough and sufficient enough to provide what we truly need.

I eventually learned that. You may remember from the first chapter, how I threw the apple at the laundry room door, spraying apple pieces across the ceiling and walls. For many months, I watched those apple bits turn brown and rot, believing they represented my shattered marriage, a memorial to my dissatisfaction.

But eventually I realized Larry couldn't meet my needs. Only God could meet them. As I looked to my heavenly Father, I experienced love, acceptance, and fulfillment.

In tearful surrender, I washed off those rotting apple pieces. I no longer needed a memorial to my rotting marriage. Once my focus released Larry from the unrealistic expectation of making me fulfilled and happy, I could choose to love Larry unconditionally. I was set free.

During that time, I noticed an attitude change in Kathy. She started using some of the communication techniques referred to in this chapter. More of our discussions and disagreements were less contentious. The more secure Kathy felt in the Lord, the more confidently she expressed her needs in a healthy manner. The demanding was gone. Her credibility was improved. I couldn't ignore her new, reasonable approaches in drawing me closer to her. This made me more receptive to her sharing, and it made the environment more conducive for me to change. I began seeing that our marriage could improve and grow, and both of us would reap the benefits. When we used these techniques, the deep conflicts of the past became manageable disagreements.

Have you washed off the rotting pieces of your bitterness and disappointment? Surrender that area now and commit yourself to resisting the idea that you can change your mate. Place her unlovely behavior in God's hands, and then keep your eyes focused on him. He longs to heal your discontent and meet your needs with his unconditional love.

Chapter 7

Serving and Leading

"Larry, look!" I pointed to the small pierced-earring jewelry box in the department store. "It's just what I've been wanting."

"Kathy, you don't need that," Larry replied. "Let's go."

I've really been trying to submit to Larry since we got married a year ago, I thought, perplexed. *But I really need this. I'm going to buy it!* But a nagging thought confused me: *Am I being disobedient to God?*

As we drove home, I wondered whether this would undermine the security of my marriage. I felt guilty and disobedient. "Oh, Lord, please forgive me if I'm wrong," I prayed, "but I just don't see why I can't spend my own money on something I need."

I couldn't see why this little thing was so important to Kathy. I merely shared my obviously insightful opinion over its uselessness. Kathy interpreted my remark as a command. As a Driver, I have an opinion about everything, even a jewelry box! If she had asked me, "Honey, are you telling me not to buy it or are you just expressing your opinion?" I would have said, "It's just a suggestion. Buy it if you want."

Submission is often a ridiculed concept in Christian circles, yet God clearly desires us to practice it. "Be subject to one another in the fear of Christ" is the primary, ideal goal—for everyone to be servants to everyone else. But our selfishness gets in the way; therefore, God establishes further guidelines: "Wives, submit to your husbands as to the Lord. For the husband is the head of the wife as Christ is the head of the church, his body, of which he is the Savior. Now as the church submits to Christ, so also wives should submit to their husbands in everything. Husbands, love your wives, just as Christ loved the church and gave himself up for her" (Eph. 5:22-25). Then in verse 33 he commands: "However, each one of you also must love his wife as he loves himself, and the wife must respect her husband."

We often define submission as an attitude of the yielded, cooperative heart that communicates a wife's desire to follow her husband's leadership. In *Romancing the Home,* author Ed Young explains, "Submission is a military word that means 'to line up according to rank,' or 'to be under the authority of.' A wife who is submissive to her husband is not saying in any way that she is inferior to him in intellect, wisdom, insight, or reason. The word relates more to function than status, and in the home, God places the weight of responsibility and accountability squarely on the shoulders of the husband."

A wife submitting to her husband and a husband loving his wife as his own body are in alignment with the needs of men and women. In *Effective Biblical Counseling,* Christian psychologist Dr. Lawrence Crabb, Jr.,

writes, "The most basic need [of every
sense of personal worth, an acceptance of
whole, real person. The two required inputs
cance (purpose, importance, adequacy for a)
ingfulness, impact) and *security* (love uncondi_ ... and
consistently expressed; permanent acceptance). My experience suggests that although men and women need both
kinds of input, for men the *primary* route to personal
worth is significance and for women the *primary* route
is security."

How It Works

Recently, I was studying John 10:1, which says,
"Truly, truly, I say to you, he who does not enter
by the door into the fold of the sheep, but climbs up
some other way, he is a thief and a robber" (NASB). I
wanted to learn more about "the fold of the sheep" and
I found some information in *Manners and Customs of
the Bible:*

> In this beautiful figure, reference is made to the
> place of shelter for the sheep where they might
> repose at night, and be safe from the attacks of
> wild beasts. The modern sheep-folds of Syria,
> which no doubt resemble those of ancient times,
> are low, flat buildings opening into a court, which
> is surrounded by a stone wall, protected on top
> by a layer of thorns.

As I read that description, I related the thorns to submission. Submission looks ugly and painful, just like those
thorns. But just as the thorns protect the sheep within the

..d, submission protects a wife from the wolves (and serpents) of temptation, of emotionally rushing into decisions before considering her husband's logical perspective.

I can look back over our many years of marriage and see how God protected me from making many unwise choices by leading me to confer with Larry first. I wasn't always thrilled about his advice, and I sometimes fought it, but for the most part his perspective was valid.

 Ed Young explains it this way in *Romancing the Home:*

> Marriage is not a business arrangement where the husband holds 51 percent of the stock and the wife 49 percent. It is a one-flesh relationship where both parties confer, fully expressing their opinions, ideas, and desires. More often than not, there is agreement either initially or eventually, but when there is not, someone must make the call. This responsibility is the man's. And when the decision is made, the wife, if she is subject to her husband, supports that decision. Right or wrong, good or bad, she says, "I'm with you to the end. You've decided. I will follow." Then she does so fully and joyfully. That is submission.

In our relationship, that is lived out in the following way: When we are faced with a decision, we talk together, each sharing our opinions, desires, and ideas. Since our natural inclination during this time is to mentally prepare our defense while the other is speaking, we'll employ the A-B Method of Communication (see Chapter 6) to guarantee that we are truly listening and hearing. Such true communication will give each of us the knowledge we are truly being heard. When we are truly heard, we are much more capable of cooperating with each other.

Once all the points have been discussed, we look for compromise. If it's an area that calls for negotiation, that can be a valid tool. This should be done on both sides of the issue. It can also be helpful to write down in columns the different issues and disagreements that we are addressing.

After we've gone through this process of give and take, there may still be disagreement. Ideally, we'll stop and delay a decision. Waiting and being in prayer for further guidance may bring agreement. If time pressures do not allow that, or it seems that agreement is impossible, then the responsibility for the final decision falls on Larry.

There have been times that we've gone through that process and I haven't agreed with Larry's decision. I haven't always been able to have the joyful attitude Ed Young talks about. But I have seen God's faithfulness in working in Larry's heart or in changing the circumstances.

What Submission Is Not

Though Ed Young encourages a wife to fully and joyfully submit, there are limitations to that attitude when abuse is occurring.

Love can be defined as "choosing the highest good for another person." "Highest good" does *not* mean allowing oneself to be attacked verbally or physically. God does not approve of a husband using the concept of submission to force a battered wife to stay in an abusive situation or to abuse the children. If you're wondering whether you're being abused, or if you are concerned your children may be at risk, seek out a professional Christian counselor or pastor. And if you are being abused, seek the help and support you need to make a wise choice: removing yourself from that situation.

If you believe your husband is not being abusive, but he doesn't show you respect or belittles you verbally, you can calmly refuse to allow him to talk to you that way. I remember calling a friend of mine on the phone. After her husband answered, he called out to her gruffly, "The phone's for you!" When she asked who it was, he said in a mean tone, "How do I know? Come get the stupid phone."

She could have said something like, "I won't allow you to talk to me like that. I feel belittled with that tone of voice." Such a response will not clear away all problems, but it could begin building strength to refuse poor treatment.

If there is no abuse in a relationship, then a wife can be submissive, knowing God will defend her needs. Through her submission, she will meet her husband's need for significance. As she does, he quite often will be more motivated to meet *her* needs.

Helping Your Husband Feel Significant

There are four ways a wife can help her huband feel significant: being his ally, admirer, advisor, and agree-er.

Be his ally. Genesis 2:18 tells us where this idea came from. "Then the Lord God said, It is not good for the man to be alone; I will make him a helper suitable for him" (NASB). When we look at the word *suitable,* we might think of a tailor measuring a beautiful new wool suit. He tucks and lets out different parts of the fabric so the suit fits perfectly. The perfect suit becomes a helper, an ally, in helping the wearer be successful.

To be a husband's "helpmate" and ally, wives need to respond in a way that "fits" him. Here are some suggestions for understanding and responding to your mate according to his temperament. (For a husband reading this chapter, these suggestions also apply to your wife.)

If your spouse is an Analytical: Roger is an Analytical and he craves creative tenderness. (Women are generally known for wanting creative tenderness, but an Analytical male can desire it as well.) Last Christmas, Roger bought Nancie, his wife, several classic books. Nancie told us, "Can you believe it? He bought me books, and he knows I don't read very much. I think he wanted these titles himself and got them for me."

Roger knew he would never get what he valued from Nancie because, as a Driver, she doesn't think of classical books as important. How much better if Nancie would understand Roger's needs and if Roger could buy her something she actually wanted. Submission means meeting a spouse's needs even when we don't value that particular need.

With an Analytical, try to avoid rushing the decision-making process and stick to specifics. Take your time, but be persistent and accurate. Let him be right when possible. Say, "What would happen if . . . ?" to encourage him to talk and think at higher levels of abstraction. Also, help him relax.

If your spouse is an Amiable: An Amiable's obvious need is peace and quiet. His underlying need is a sense of value as a person.

Mike is an Amiable and his wife, Diane, is a Driver. Diane had begun a very successful aerobics business about the same time Mike was working on his dissertation. Mike says, "I wasn't providing for my family financially, and my self-esteem plummeted. I had no energy to spend on my relationship with Diane."

Diane: "I could see Mike struggling and I felt so distant from him. I asked him over and over again, 'What can I do?' He always said, 'I don't know.' The further apart we drifted, the more I became convinced Mike didn't want me so involved in my business. I wanted him to express it, but he wouldn't. So I initiated our having lunch together once a week. We also worked through Willard Harley's book *His Needs/Her Needs*. That book helped me see how much Mike needed me to be his ally. During one of our lunches, I asked him directly if he wanted me to continue in my business. He said no. The Lord gave me such a tremendous sense of peace and freedom that I knew I must let go of my business."

Mike: "About that time, I'd been able to get a job in California, but that would mean a big move for us. Diane didn't want our children raised in the southern California lifestyle, but eventually she said with a sweet spirit, 'Do whatever you think is best.' When she gave me permission to make the decision, I felt energized. I knew she valued me. Her biblical submission empowered me to have confidence in my decision-making capabilities."

Diane concludes, "We've been living in California for a while now, and God has opened up doors for me to be a professional personal physical trainer. He gave me back my desired business and strengthened our marriage through my submission to him and Michael."

Don't offer an Amiable options and don't debate facts or data. Don't demand quick responses but do support him in his feelings. Show interest in him as a person and watch for hurt feelings. Finally, and most important, encourage him to take leadership and risks.

If your spouse is a Driver: A Driver's obvious need is control and productivity. His underlying need is appreciation for his endeavors. A Driver loves to be in control but prefers to delegate responsibility.

Driver Mike, who is married to Sonia, an Analytical, didn't want involvement in all the details. But Sonia was raised in a Latino family where the husband was involved in every single decision. "I wanted Mike to help me make every decision," Sonia says.

"I wanted to be in charge but felt bogged down with all these details," Mike says. "I wanted my wife to be my peer rather than my servant, constantly looking to me for advice. I didn't want to make *all* those decisions. It didn't dawn on me at first that we were struggling with cultural differences. Later, we had to work things out to become more equal."

Ask a Driver about specifics, and praise the results he achieves, not his personality. Don't waste his time, and do be well organized. Compliment his leadership, but don't tell him what to do. Encourage him to be aware of his own feelings and sensitive to the needs of others. And most important: encourage him to release control.

If your spouse is an Expressive: An Expressive's obvious need is fun and excitement. His underlying need is constant encouragement and approval.

Peter is an Expressive and his wife, Shirley, is an Amiable. She notes, "Peter was so attractive to me because of his outgoing nature, but at times I get so tired of cheering him on. Yet when I am his cheerleader, I know it meets his needs and I really want to do that."

Peter says, "I appreciate Shirley's attentiveness. Even though I try to be sensitive to her need for peace and quiet, I just love getting all caught up in some new project, like raising money for an organization. Shirley is excellent at calmly pointing out the disadvantages of some of these things and helping me keep a balance. I guess I'm open to her input because she usually points out the positive as well as the negative. Plus, I know she'll abide by my final decision."

Use strong technical language, and don't bore an Expressive with details. Support his dreams and intuitions, asking his opinions about people. Develop mutually exciting ideas, and compliment his creativity. Encourage him to set goals and reach them.

Be his admirer. Admiration and respect are the second loving tools a woman has to make her husband feel significant. As Diane noted earlier in this chapter, admiration is always an Amiable husband's greatest need, and it carries equal importance for most men.

I have spoken to countless wounded men who share the same story: The cutting, sarcastic, and unsympathetic words from their wives have left scars on their hearts and sapped them of strength to take leadership in their families. I am amazed how many women do not realize the power of their words. (And that goes for men as well.)

Harsh, ungrateful words wear down a man's resolve to take leadership. On the other hand, encouraging words from an appreciative wife will bolster a man's spirit and make him feel admired.

A wife may have difficulty giving admiration because she's afraid praise will prevent him from finishing the task. Yet, "I appreciate your doing that" is more of a motivator than, "It's about time you worked on that."

Proverbs 14:1 (NASB) tells us, "The wise woman builds her house, but the foolish tears it down with her own hands." Here are some ways wives might be tearing down their husband's significance:

- Comparing. Telling him about the neighborhood friend who always has his garage clean will not inspire your husband to do the same.

- Arguing. Not accepting his final decision will just make him fearful of making decisions (especially for Amiables) or more determined to get his way in the future (especially Drivers).

- Correcting him in public. You may think rehearsing his faults will change him, but it will only hurt his feelings and de-energize him.

- Teasing sensitive areas. A friend of ours made a joke about her husband's paunch in front of us, and his face fell in disappointment.

- Expecting perfection. It's sometimes easy to think we can't give admiration until he "performs" a task one hundred percent correctly. Instead, appreciate what he's done as he goes along.

Here are ways to build up rather than tear down.

Listen and don't interrupt. A woman tends to "over-lap" in conversation, talking while someone else is talking. This is acceptable with a group of women, but it makes a man feel put down and unappreciated. A wife must focus on listening to all he says. She can ask questions that let him know she has listened.

Keep confidences. Only tell someone else after you've asked his permission. Don't ask for prayer for an unsaved husband (or one who isn't growing spiritually) by going into detail about all his faults and problems.

Value his opinion.

There have been many times in our marriage when I've hesitated asking Larry's opinion because I'm afraid he will disagree with what I want to do. But most of the time, his logical and wise perspective is a great advantage to consider, even if he does disagree with me.

Now, in the margin of this page, write out ten qualities, skills, or talents that you admire in your mate, and concentrate on praising and appreciating them. Bob Turnbull says: "No man tells his wife to be quiet when she's saying how wonderful he is."

Be his advisor. With all the "positives" we've been talking about, you may be wondering whether a wife is ever meant to express her needs or give her opinion. She certainly is! Depending on a husband's security and significance level, he will be more open or resistant to his wife being his advisor. A wife must respond to her husband depending upon his level of maturity and how much he can receive.

I often say that I'm all for submitting to my husband; that is, submitting all my ideas and opinions for us to make a decision together! Early in our marriage, especially during that time of conflict, I didn't regard Larry as being very open to my opinion or feelings. But as we healed and matured, he became more open to my ideas. Now he considers all my opinions as we talk about the decisions we must make.

I highly value Kathy's opinions and perspective. Together we consider the pros and cons of any decision. If, after our dialogue, we are not in agreement, we may wait awhile and talk about it again. But I know Kathy will support me in the end.

Recently, as we turned Darcy's bedroom into our office after she moved out on her own, we discussed the kind of lighting we wanted. Kathy expressed her fears that my lighting plans wouldn't be sufficient for her. I assured her they would, and she acquiesced, not quite convinced. I promised her that if the lighting wasn't what I expected, we would do whatever was necessary to correct it and meet her needs. That was an acceptable compromise, and I appreciated her bowing to my plans.

When you share your ideas and feelings (using "I" messages, as described in Chapter 6), be careful about your tone of voice. Is it condescending or critical, even though your words aren't?

Sarah didn't understand that the way she was responding to her husband, Stephen, was unsatisfactory. When Stephen would start to raise his voice, Sarah would reply in a very syrupy, calm, and controlled tone, "Now, Stephen. Calm down. You know this isn't that important." Without her realizing it, her tone communicated that he was inferior for getting upset and she was superior because she was in control of her emotions.

A better response would be, "Stephen, I know you're really feeling upset right now. It upsets me too, so let's talk about it." It wouldn't even hurt for her to have a little frenzy or frustration in her own voice. When we know someone is identifying with our feelings, and feeling that way too, our frustration is more easily dissolved than if she communicates, "You shouldn't be feeling that way."

Be his agree-er. Even when a wife has been her husband's ally, admirer, and advisor, there will still be times when couples won't agree. Then she must choose to be his agree-er, as long as it isn't abusive or involves sin. She can still say something like, "Honey, I don't completely agree with your decision, but I will do what you say."

At the same time, there is a difference between submission and obedience. A woman can be obedient, but she may not be submissive. Obedience is when she does what her husband says while her heart fights his leading every step of the way. Submission can be defined as "an attitude of love that desires to cooperate." Although she may not be able to feel thrilled about her husband's decision, she needs to guard against bitterness. Otherwise, she may be obeying, but not submitting.

The crux of a wife's ability to submit is her level of

trust in God. Entrusting herself to God's sovereignty and care will enable her to be her husband's agree-er. Psalm 50:15 says, "I want you to trust me in your times of trouble, so I can rescue you, and you can give me glory" (TLB). She can also claim Proverbs 21:1 and substitute "husband" for "king": "The king's heart is in the hand of the Lord; he directs it like a watercourse wherever he pleases."

God is in control! By making your husband feel significant with the support of his plans, along with expressing your goals and desires, you'll build him into that man of security and maturity God desires.

As we've talked about making a husband feel significant, we hope you've identified ways that you can be your mate's ally, admirer, advisor, and agree-er. We can't guarantee that he'll become everything you need him to be, but God does promise to be in control and work within your marriage. Trust him! He is worthy of that honor.

For Men Only

What about the husband's responsibility to the wife? I've had to learn a lot about what that means. When I was first married, I didn't give much thought to the concept of submission. I just assumed Kathy would submit to my direction for our family. I didn't spend too much time trying to provide leadership, however. I was too busy chasing my own dreams and trying to fill the vacancies of my own life.

After healing came to our marriage, I realized how often I had been either passive and dropped the ball of leadership or charged ahead seeking my own goals.

Now I seek Kathy's counsel. I depend on her opinions and find that our joint decision making gives us the best results. However, I know that God holds me ultimately accountable for the choices we make as a family. As Raymond C. Ortlund, Jr., says in *Recovering Biblical Manhood and Womanhood*, "In the partnership of two spiritually equal human beings, man and woman, the man bears the primary responsibility to lead the partnership in a God-glorifying direction."

We husbands are commanded:

> For the husband is the head of the wife, as Christ also is the head of the church, he himself being the Savior of the body. But as the church is subject to Christ, so also the wives ought to be to their husbands in everything. Husbands, love your wives, just as Christ also loved the church and gave himself up for her. So husbands ought also to love their own wives as their own bodies. He who loves his own wife loves himself. (Eph. 5:23-24, 28; NASB)

Colossians 3:19 (also NASB) instructs us: "Husbands, love your wives, and do not be embittered against them."

Our instructions are summed up in two words: service and love. Leadership does not mean dictatorship. Leadership calls us to be sensitive to our wives' needs. Pastor Jack Hayford says, "God's plan is for a man to take his leadership role to learn of, to accept, and to exercise those responsibilities (not privileges) that thereby he might serve and assist God's means for the release of a woman's highest potential."

I often wonder how some men believe they should

govern all the details of life for their wife and children. Such men do not respect their wives or consider their opinions valuable and worthy of their attention. Male domination and control that seeks its own interests and demands its own way is sinful and unbiblical.

Men who act like this are often motivated by the lie many believe: that our *worth* is directly tied to our *role*. Many men confuse personal weakness with a willingness to yield their views to others'. Yet Scripture clearly teaches that our value comes from our position in Christ. At the same time, God does ask us men to exercise our headship. What does that really look like?

Valuing. A husband leads and serves by considering his wife's opinion important through listening to her and having discussions with her. We husbands show ourselves to be secure in our self-esteem when we're not threatened by our wives' opinions.

First Peter 3:7 reads, "Husbands, in the same way be considerate as you live with your wives, and treat them with respect as the weaker partner as heirs with you of the gracious gift of life, so that nothing will hinder your prayers." That word "respect" means "attach high value to." When you and I listen and are open to our wives' ideas, we are "attaching high value to them."

We each look at life as though through one eye: our own perspective. But if we will consider our wives' ideas as a second "eye," we can truly see with 20/20 vision. Proverbs 12:15 (NASB) tells us, "The way of a fool is right in his own eyes, but a wise man is he who listens to counsel."

I wasn't looking for counsel from anyone—especially Kathy—in my early marriage. I thought I needed to convince her of the error of her ways. It wasn't that I didn't think she had good ideas; it was just that mine were more "important." So whenever she tried to share her opinions, I debated her until she surrendered—usually in tears.

Now I see the value of Kathy's ideas. We make decisions together, although I know that if we come to an impasse, Kathy will yield to me. But that's pressure right from God because I know he will hold me accountable! Bunny Wilson says, "When I first began to practice submission in my marriage, my husband said it put the fear of God in his heart."

I'm convinced now that as we husbands consider our wives' perspective, we aren't weak, but wise—wise in receiving the counsel of others. And what better person to offer that counsel than the woman who loves us more than anyone else and wants the best for us?

Serving. As I look back, I can remember a time when I failed to provide leadership. When our children were very young, Kathy suggested organizing a family devotional time. I realized it would be a good idea, so after dinner one night I began our new family tradition. I kept it simple and short, but within a few minutes the squirming wee ones lost interest and began interrupting. I got frustrated and tried to snap them back into shape. But our time together still unraveled. So much for devotions that evening! I tried again another night, only again to face failure. That was the last time I initiated family devotions. My Driver temperament couldn't handle not being able to control the situation.

I now deeply regret my lack of spiritual leadership in that situation. I should have been patient, waited out the interruptions, stuck to the plan. Kathy had some simple suggestions to improve our time together, but when they didn't create the quick results I desired, I just gave up. We never did establish that precious family tradition.

Headship leads through patience and perseverance. Headship understands that progress must often be measured with a micrometer instead of a yardstick.

It is from our failures that we learn our greatest lessons. Unpleasant experiences shape us. They give us a foundation to build strong and decisive victories in the future. That's what happened for me.

A couple of years ago, I heard Bishop Wellington Boone speak at the Promise Keepers event in Los Angeles. He made one comment that revolutionized my marriage. He was encouraging us to lead our wives when he referred to his marriage and said: "I will never let her out-serve me again." I barely heard the rest of his talk. The Lord seemed to impress on me the truth that for the twenty-five years of our marriage, Kathy had truly out-served me. I realized the strongest hand I could play in my role as a sensitive spiritual leader could only be dealt from the top of the deck, and that deck was called "service."

I thought of the servant role Jesus modeled for me. In the Phillips translation of Mark 10:42-44, Jesus says, "You know that the so-called rulers in the world lord it over them, and their great men have absolute power. But it must not be so among you. No, whoever among you wants to be great, must become the servant . . . for the Son of Man himself has not come to be served, but to serve."

That day I went home to Kathy and said to her, "I appreciate the support you've given me all these years. I recognize the sacrifices you've made and know you've submitted to my poor choices many times. Those failures and successes have sculpted me into the man I am today, and I'm very grateful that you have been an integral part of my growth."

As Kathy looked at me with stunned surprise, I continued, "I pledge, as of today, to out-serve you. I want to give you even more reason to submit to my leadership because I am a man desiring to be a godly husband."

I was truly amazed by Larry's declaration. And in all honesty, I expected it to be short-lived. But it wasn't. He became even more attentive to my needs. He began doing the grocery shopping weekly. He more quickly responded to my requests for help around the house. He eagerly asked me how he could serve me.

Our favorite joke became a contest. "I'm out-serving you," one of us would say. And then the other would counter, "No, I'm out-serving you."

The next year, I was preparing to attend another PK event when Kathy grabbed my arm and said to me, "A year ago you pledged to out-serve me. Honey, you have truly done it. I love you so much." She followed that with one of the most tender kisses we have ever shared.

Men, we are just beginning to discover the real secret to leadership. Each day I struggle with choices to please myself or honor God's design for a godly man. I thought I was making good progress—until I discovered another husband who took this concept a step further.

Sally Conway's Gift

 Our friend Jim Conway sent us a letter in February 1997, updating his prayer partners on the care of his wife, Sally, who was seriously ill with cancer. She would see the Lord face-to-face four months later.

He wrote, "One of my New Year's resolutions in January 1995 was a promise to God that I would see Sally safely through this life. And God in his great love to me and Sally is giving us the opportunity to spend lots of time together. I'm glad God didn't take her quickly.

Apparently the bone cancer has spread throughout her spine and into her arms, legs, shoulders, and neck. For some months now, she has had little or no leg mobility. Now she is also gradually losing arm mobility.

"When Sally drops off to sleep, I scramble to keep up with office work, the laundry, and kitchen cleanup. In the cracks, I'm reediting and updating my first book, *Men in Mid-Life Crisis.*

"When Sally is awake, she wants me to be very close to her—standing beside her, holding her hand, rubbing her back, or just talking. Sometimes I put a table next to her bed so I can touch her while I continue to work.

"I'm not taking my walks anymore. I can catch up after Sally is healed, or Jesus takes her to be with himself. This is my time to be with Sally.

"Last evening Sally said to me, 'Aren't you getting tired of this? Don't you just wish I would die?' I told her with absolute honesty, 'You are not a burden to me. In fact, it may sound strange, but you are giving me a great opportunity to serve you. It is rewarding for me to care for you, honey.'

"After I explained my feelings to Sally, her right hand started to tremble and very slowly rise off the bed. I knew she wanted to touch me. So I leaned down near her hand and she patted the side of my face.

"You ask me if I'm sacrificing? My response is, 'Not

at all!' It's true I'm tired, I'm not getting to walk, and I can't really leave the house for errands—but there will be lots of time later. Her hand pats are enough for now."

Jim took real leadership beyond service to sacrifice. If we are to treat our wives like Christ treated the church, then it seems our lives should be marked by sacrifice, not demands. We should be acting for Christ, and our lives should be marked by service, not control. Our behavior should encourage our wives to submit to our leadership—willingly and joyfully.

Chapter 8

What Says "I Love You"?

⭐ *Our fourth wedding anniversary is in a few days,* I thought as I sat down, more and more aware of my bulging stomach. I was pregnant with our first child, and I didn't feel very good about myself. It was hard to consider myself sexy or desirable; sometimes I wondered if Larry still looked at me the same way. I thought that if he would buy me flowers for our anniversary, that would prove his love for me.

As June 20 got closer and closer, my hopes for flowers increased, even though he had seldom bought me flowers. I reasoned, *He should know how important this is to me. I'm sure he'll come through.*

The day finally arrived. Unexpectedly the doorbell rang. I opened the door to find a florist's delivery man holding a beautiful spray of long-stemmed red roses. It was gorgeous! My heart beat with excitement. *He does love me,* I thought. *He actually thought of it himself!*

I was eager to open the card and see the romantic

words Larry had written. The card read, "Congratulations on choosing us to build your new pool. We know you'll love it." It was signed by the pool company we had hired the previous week.

Suddenly, I started laughing. "Lord, you do have a sense of humor. You allowed these flowers to arrive on my anniversary so I wouldn't be too disappointed when Larry arrives home empty-handed. I see now how unrealistic my thinking is."

 Recently, though, I did surprise Kathy when we were speaking at a couples' Valentine's Day banquet. At the end of our presentation, after telling the crowd about our different opinions of flowers, I pulled out an exquisite real rose, covered in 24-karat gold. As the audience clapped in delight, Kathy, totally caught off guard, let me know she was amazed by leaning over and giving me a tender kiss. That rose sits in a glass vase on Kathy's desk as a constant reminder that even we husbands can learn new tricks.

 I was thrilled with Larry's creativity. It touched me deeply and made me feel even more secure.

 Men and women have different definitions of love and romance. We each speak a different language when it comes to meeting the other's needs. This is another area where we can easily assume our spouse's definition is the same as ours.

God's kind of love is described by the word *agape.* Pastor Ed Young, in *Romancing the Home,* writes, "Agape is a self-effacing, sacrificial kind of love that is exclusive, permanent, and unconditional. Agape love is essential to marriage because conditions in any relationship change. Health, outlook, financial status—all are subject to change. If love is to survive in an atmosphere of change, it must be rooted in something that is changeless."

In order to strive for that kind of love, we need to find out how our spouse wants his or her needs met. After hearing about this "definition of love" concept, I decided to ask Larry how I made him feel loved and important. I already knew what he would say. When I asked, he would say, "Let's go to the bedroom and you can show me."

But I asked anyway: "Honey, what is it I do for you that makes you feel loved?"

I knew this was a meaningful question and I stopped to think about it. Then I said, "Why, Kath, it's what you're doing right now."

I was surprised because we weren't close to the bedroom at all! In fact, we were in the family room. Larry was lying on the couch, and I sat massaging his feet as we watched football on TV.

I realized he valued something that has no value to me. I can't stand to have anyone touch my feet—they're too ticklish. Not only that, but we were watching football—not exactly my favorite pastime! But I've learned I can do these things for him because I know it makes him feel loved and significant.

Kathy has told me many times how I make her feel loved and important: by listening and reflecting back her feelings. Now that I know the importance of conversation to Kathy, I choose to initiate it.

I have stumbled many times. Kathy would often come

to me with a concern or problem, and before she would finish talking, I had figured out the solution and offered it. After all, when I talk about a problem with someone, I'm usually looking for another opinion. But I found out Kathy didn't want an answer, a solution, or another perspective. She just wanted someone to listen.

Usually, men are expected to fix problems. It feeds our significance needs and gives purpose to our leadership role. It comes with the territory. It seems odd that someone in need would not value our precious opinion. However, most women initially want to be heard on an emotional level. It's only later, after making their true feelings known, that they're more receptive to a solution. I guess that's what Galatians 6:2 is all about. It tells believers to bear one another's burdens—not fix their problems.

Why Can't We Say What Love Means?

Even when husbands and wives understand this concept, they still often hesitate to share their needs and wants. Here are two reasons why.

If I express my romantic visions, I'll sound selfish. Obviously, a person who exclusively thinks of his own needs *is* selfish and should face his sinful mindset. But since God intends the marriage relationship as a way to meet those needs, it's not wrong to express them.

Expressing our need for romance is not wrong. But if we become bitter or resentful over our mate's inattention, then we've demonstrated our own insecurity.

If I tell you what I want and you respond, your actions don't count.

Leslie is typical of the many women I listen to during private counseling sessions when I speak at women's retreats. "I so much want Jeff to arrange romantic times," she told me, as tears dribbled down her cheeks. "I daydream about walking on the beach with him or having a picnic at our local park."

Gently I inquired, "Have you told Jeff what you want?"

Leslie looked at me with surprise. "Oh, no. If I have to tell him what to do, it doesn't have as much meaning. Then I'd feel like I'd forced him to do it."

For a long time, I felt the same way. But this perspective is a corollary to the myth that our husbands can read our minds.

Judy, a woman who has learned to express her romantic needs, gives us the better outlook. "I realize that my husband appreciates my romantic suggestions. It's not that he doesn't want to meet my needs; he simply doesn't think about it. I can value what he does for me because he chooses to do it and it requires his energy."

What's Your Love Style?

Besides different definitions of love, there are also a variety of people's "styles" in giving and receiving love. Some give gifts and cards, others verbally express their feelings. Some spouses communicate their love through providing financially, while others do it more subtly, through being a "cheerleader" for their spouse's activities, for example. There are always those who touch, kiss, and hug to express their love. And some also call it love when they have high expectations for their loved one's success.

Of course, we can be a combination of these categories. As with the temperaments, none of these perceptions of love is incorrect or wrong. The difficulty comes when we expect everyone else to express love the same way we do and feel hurt or rejected if they don't. Has your spouse been one of these "lovers," yet you haven't received her type of love *as* love? Could you expand your thinking to include other styles or choose to respond in a way that your spouse will value?

Our friend Pamala Kennedy tells how, as an Expressive, she longed for huge birthday parties with all her friends in attendance. Since her husband, Richard, didn't do that for her, she did it for him year after year. Little did she realize that her Analytical husband wanted a quiet evening out for just the two of them on his birthday. Once she recognized what temperament and love category they each were, she stopped having huge birthday parties for Richard and took him to a quaint bed and breakfast for an overnight private party. Just the two of them.

Here are some further ways to evaluate whether you're communicating the love you want to give and the love you want to receive.

Involvement and interest. Generally speaking, men want their wives to enjoy sports and recreation with them. On the other hand, women want love expressed by husbands taking initiative in the home.

When a husband pays attention to the children, usually his wife feels loved. Mary Jo longed for her husband, Doug, to spend more time with their son, twelve-year-old Timmy. Doug repeatedly said he would but didn't follow through. One evening, Mary Jo cried out to the Lord,

"Father, I've tried everything I know to bring them together, but nothing has worked. I give up. By faith, I trust you know what's best for them both and will fulfill it."

That night, as Doug and Mary Jo cuddled in bed, she heard him say, "I was thinking on the way home from work today that I'd like to spend more time with Timmy. I think I'll ask him if he'd like to learn to play tennis with me."

Mary Jo couldn't believe her ears. With fresh tears running down her cheeks, she told Doug about her surrender of her expectations earlier in the evening.

Doug's commitment began a love of tennis that he and Timmy enjoy to this day. Whenever they go out for a game of tennis, Mary Jo feels loved.

Responsiveness and action. We all can feel loved when our spouse responds to our suggestions or requests. Sometimes we err in judging the depth of their love based on the quickness of their response.

At times, we women interpret love by how often and quickly our husbands take action in giving us affection. When Larry and I were dating, Larry frequently held my hand, put his arm around me, and made me feel loved and important. When he expressed his love in that way publicly, I felt secure.

After we were married, my Prince Charming rarely held my hand or put his arm around me. I was shocked. I began keeping track of how often he failed to hold my hand. That only made me bitter.

After the wedding, who in their right mind would prefer holding hands to making love? I believed affection before marriage was just the means to getting the "real stuff" later, and somehow sex would replace the inferior hand holding. However, over the years I've learned to enjoy giving Kathy the affection she needs and deserves.

Now that I understand Larry's perspective, I don't take it personally anymore. I've also realized that it's all right for me to take Larry's hand and remind him that it's important to me. Larry has been a good student, as he now rarely passes by me at home without reaching out to touch me.

Giving gifts. The Expressive woman, in particular, is the lover of this category. She thrives on cards, gifts, and fun times together.

Karen and Dana, an Expressive wife and an Amiable husband, have gone over this area many times in their fifteen-year marriage. Karen says, "When we were dating, Dana would bring me a rose at school and celebrate each month anniversary of our dating. I was thrilled. But since we've been married, he doesn't express his love in those ways very often. He knows how much it means to me, why doesn't he do it all the time?"

Dana gazes calmly at Karen as she shares her romantic visions, then he shrugs. It takes a lot of energy to do all that, and often that's more energy than an Amiable has available. "Besides," he says, "if I did those things routinely, she would take them for granted."

Another man feels he shows his love by no longer joining the guys for drinking after work. But because he doesn't tell his wife "I love you" or buy her gifts, she goes to a marriage counselor, convinced he has stopped loving her. Although she values his not drinking any more, he has not specifically explained that he stopped doing it for her. It isn't until the counselor hears both sides of their story that he is able to point out the love each was expressing.

Showing support.

 We all want our spouse to support us. But even this has different definitions for each one of us. As I was growing up, I really valued my parents' participation in my school activities and social events. That spelled love to me, and I intended to give that same kind of love to my children.

 I didn't feel particularly more valued or loved when my parents attended my functions at school. That didn't become my definition of love. Kathy would get upset with me when I didn't attend our children's school or sports activities. I didn't regard it as important. But because that spelled love to Kathy, she believed I wasn't expressing love to our children. I wanted to demonstrate my love for them differently, in ways that meant love to me.

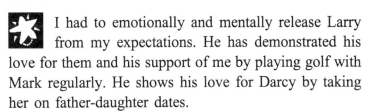 I had to emotionally and mentally release Larry from my expectations. He has demonstrated his love for them and his support of me by playing golf with Mark regularly. He shows his love for Darcy by taking her on father-daughter dates.

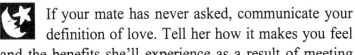 If your mate has never asked, communicate your definition of love. Tell her how it makes you feel and the benefits she'll experience as a result of meeting your needs. Then be grateful for whatever steps she takes toward what is meaningful to you, whether it's exactly

what you desire or not. Encouragement and gratitude, not criticism, will motivate her to do even more. And, of course, don't assume you know her definition of love. Ask, then fulfill it.

We began this chapter by talking about roses and Larry's creativity in presenting me with that golden rose several years ago. More recently, he further amazed me when, for two consecutive Christmases, he brought me a dozen long-stemmed roses, first red, then white. The white ones came with a card that said: "Red ones last year, white ones this year. My love, every year, Larry."

Chapter 9

Fear of Feelings

This retreat better be worth all the hassle it takes to get ready, I thought, as three-year-old Darcy followed at my heels, whining about wanting a cookie. I had really been looking forward to attending this couples' retreat with Larry and hoped it would be a breakthrough for our relationship. I wouldn't allow myself to face my true opinion. But I feared that if this didn't reunite us, nothing would.

That evening, as we neared the freeway exit for the retreat center, Larry said, "How about if we just keep driving and spend some time alone down in San Diego?"

Panic made my heart jump. I wanted to scream, "Don't you dare back out of this! This is our only hope." Instead, I gulped back my fear and replied, "No, honey, we've committed to this. Let's go."

I was relieved when Larry didn't argue.

I really didn't see the sense of going on this retreat. Wasn't our marriage just fine? When I compared it to my friends', it seemed pretty good. But I'd promised Kathy we'd go.

I still couldn't believe how that promise had come about. Kathy and I had made love one evening several months earlier, and it was so significant to me that I told her, "I'll give you whatever you want," thinking she might want to buy some new clothes.

I was surprised when she answered, "I want us to go on a couples' retreat." That wasn't what I had in mind. Now I was stuck, and Kathy wouldn't let me convince her to go to San Diego instead.

When the presentations started at the retreat, I was surprised at the approach the speakers took. They talked a lot about feelings. Feelings! Of what importance was that? I had come to learn about marriage.

But as the weekend progressed, my eyes were slowly opened to the importance of sharing the real me with Kathy through feelings. As Kathy gently shared her feelings of frustration, I learned of the unintentional pain I caused her. For the first time I heard things from her heart that gripped me in ways I could not ignore. I began to see how a root of selfishness and rigid opinions closed me off from being the real leader Kathy needed and desired.

But getting in touch with my feelings was harder than I'd expected. I realized that, as a man and as a policeman, I squelched any and every feeling I might experience. My Driver temperament made it even more difficult. When feelings surfaced, the unpleasant ones threatened my sense of control. Then it finally occurred to me: I feared feelings. I was ashamed and knew I must face that fear.

Instinctively I knew God had created me with feelings. Being a healthy and whole man required digging them up. I knew it wasn't going to be easy, but I began to see that the "real man" image of the Marlboro Man cheated me from being all of who I really was.

So I decided I would try to uncover this elusive ability God had given me. The small successes I achieved on the weekend were immediately rewarded by seeing Kathy's love for me blossom. I actually began to enjoy sharing my feelings with her. I could see God's touch of healing upon our marriage. The unity and joy we'd had in the beginning of our relationship was returning. I was as thrilled as Kathy. But I still struggled with exposing those feelings.

 Generally speaking, women have a hard time comprehending most men's unspoken attitude: "I don't have feelings. Let's just talk about opinions and facts." But women want to have their hearts listened to, not just their minds. They want to hear and know what's going on in their husband's heart. And they long to have him encourage them at an emotional level.

Why are feelings such a difficult area for many men? Let's look at two reasons why men have difficulty recognizing their feelings and allowing themselves to react emotionally.

My Dad Never Cried, Why Should I?

 Few men had fathers who shed a tear, even at a funeral. It not only wasn't modeled, it wasn't considered manly. Instead, the "macho" ideal for men pervaded most male thinking. As a result, feelings were considered wimpy. I now recognize that this nation and its marriages need men who will model a healthier viewpoint about feelings.

In *How to Bring Out the Best in Your Spouse*, H. Norman Wright explains, "A man expects to be in control, not to lose control. He's expected to be confident and assertive, not afraid, hesitant, anxious, insecure, or sad. He's supposed to be sufficient and know what he's doing; rational and analytical, not passive, dependent, bewildered, or in need of support or comfort. Men are well aware of these expectations and try to live up to them. They guard against what they must not be in the eyes of society."

For a healthy model, men can look to Jesus, who cried in public and expressed tenderness toward those who were needy. As more and more men get in touch with their emotional side, wives can encourage that change by listening closely and creating an atmosphere that encourages that kind of change. We'll talk more about that later in this chapter.

The Pressure to Share

Because men haven't been trained to express their feelings, they assume everyone else is confident on the inside and only they are experiencing feelings of inadequacy.

Then add this kink in the works. Wives may give their husbands this impression: "Unless you share your feelings with me, I'm not going to feel secure in your love. I may not even be motivated to love you in return."

Imagine how a wife would feel if her husband asked her to do something for which she had no training or experience. Then imagine how she would feel if he added, "And unless you can do it, I'm not going to feel secure in your love. In fact, I may not even be motivated to love you in return."

That would most likely make her feel tense, confused,

or angry. Maybe that's how a man feels when a wife puts pressure on him to "share now!"

"The Trance"

Because men feel threatened and vulnerable when required to share feelings, they resort to what Joan Shapiro, author of *Men: A Translation for Women,* calls "the trance." This is a withdrawal mechanism whereby men retreat to reading the newspaper, poking around the Internet, watching TV, even working in the garage for hours. They tune out the world around them.

A wife and mother has the uncanny ability to pay attention to several things at once. If she's watching TV and the baby cries in the far bedroom, she hears it immediately. She looks over at her husband, and he shows no awareness. "See how lazy he is," she concludes. "He doesn't even care enough about the baby to go take care of him."

Because *she* heard the baby, she assumes he did also. In reality, he hears nothing but the sound of the TV. He is in his trance, and nothing but a direct nudge on the shoulder will stir him out of it.

A wife may say, though, "But he's not like that on his job or when we're out in public!"

That's true. It has everything to do with what he expects from "home." In *You Just Don't Understand,* linguist Deborah Tannen explains, "For everyone, home is a place to be offstage. But the comfort of home can have opposite and incompatible meanings for women and men. For many men, the comfort of home means freedom from having to prove themselves and impress through verbal display. At last, they are in a situation where talk is not required. They are free to remain silent. But for women,

When the Honeymoon's Over

home is a place where they are free to talk, and where they feel the greatest need for talk, with those they are closest to."

A wife can ease the "threat of sharing" a husband may feel by giving him space. When he walks in the door, she can give him a chance to unwind by reading the mail, watching the news, or reading the newspaper. When he's in his trance, a wife needs to understand that it's not meant as a vehicle of expressing his disapproval or lack of love. He's "recharging" in that state of oblivion. Give him time to thaw out from the cold environment of the working world. Then follow the guidelines shared at the end of this chapter.

Why Men Fear Feelings

Many men fear feelings for the following reasons:

Unpleasant feelings mean love is dying. Danny and Terrie have gone through a lot of healing work to assure the survival of their marriage. One of the problems was Danny's inability to show positive or negative feelings. When their marriage counselor showed Danny a list of "feeling words," he was surprised at how many there were.

Danny explains, "I could only relate to ten out of the two hundred words on the list. As I worked on identifying my feelings, and even began to allow myself to experience angry feelings toward Terrie, I was terrified. In the past, we were either calm and loving, or hateful and therefore getting a divorce. When I'd hear of other couples arguing and working through their disagreement, I was amazed. I didn't know there was a middle ground. I had to learn that I could experience unpleasant feelings toward Terrie and still work through them without it meaning we were destined for divorce court."

Tom and Deborah experienced something similar. When Expressive Deborah became short-tempered because of an increased workload at the office, Tom, an Amiable, sometimes felt the brunt of it. Tom says, "I couldn't understand her reactions. I equate Deborah's anger with the meaning that she doesn't love me anymore. I'm getting better at seeing that she's actually displacing her anger from work onto me."

"I didn't mean anything by blowing off steam at home," Deborah explains. "I'm just very verbal when I'm upset and once I say it, it's over with. But I had to understand that Tom didn't view it that way. Now I'm learning to deal with it more constructively."

Unpleasant feelings equal conflict. This is especially true of the Amiable, but to some degree it applies to most men. As we've seen, most men think that discussing the relationship must mean something's wrong, whereas most women think that talking is a key to marital health.

Wayne, an Amiable, wants peace at any cost. When he hears Vickie asking him to share his feelings about their relationship, he easily slips into what Vickie calls his "turtle mode." He withdraws emotionally and physically, interpreting her request as what he calls "sniper fire." He sees it as a personal attack. Lacking the energy to continue the discussion, Wayne counters, "I can't handle this anymore right now. Let's talk more tomorrow."

Analytical Vickie loves to have long, detailed conversations and interprets this plea for peace as lack of interest in her personally. She says, "When Wayne slipped into his 'turtle' reaction, that was evidence he didn't care for me. I believed that if our relationship was important to him, he would want to talk about strengthening our marriage. As a result, I'd get angry and I'd confront him by saying something like, 'That's right. Just go ahead and crawl into your shell.'"

Wayne feels hurt by her comment. Growing up, he was often belittled by his Driver mother and learned to withhold his feelings or opinions for fear she would use them against him. When Vickie reacts in anger, he withdraws as if his mother was berating him.

When Vickie realized her anger made Wayne feel like she was belittling him as his mother had, she began to respond more compassionately and tenderly toward him. She has learned to say, "Yes, we do have a conflict, but it's not the end of the world. We're in this together for the long term. Tomorrow can be peaceful if we deal with it now."

How *Not* to Get Your Man to Open Up

When the man in your life doesn't share his feelings with you, resist these destructive responses:

1. Create a scene with anger in order to get any reaction from him.
2. Keep asking over and over again, "How do you feel?" until it becomes nagging.
3. Try to make him feel guilty by accusing, "You never share your feelings with me."
4. Share an abundance of your own feelings continual so that you'll show him how to share feelings. H. Norman Wright advises, "Think of it as speaking your language to someone from a non-English-speaking culture. Overloading another person tends to short-circuit their response."

5. If he does try to share his feelings, say, "Well, it's about time."
6. Secretly pray he doesn't learn to share his feelings so that you can continue to complain with other wives about insensitive husbands.
7. React with self-righteousness because you're convinced you're more progressively enlightened about emotions.

Creating the Climate for Openness

Bob credits Yvonne with developing an atmosphere in their home that invited him to share his feelings. Yvonne says, "Bob had been abandoned as a child and was raised in foster homes where he was neglected and abused, sometimes left in closets. When we married, there was a big wall around him and no expression of feelings."

"I was also a policeman for a time," Bob says, "and that vocation taught me never to reveal emotions. But after we'd been married for some time, I began to feel more secure with Yvonne. I knew she wasn't going to leave and abandon me."

Yvonne goes on: "At first when he'd say, 'Let's talk,' I saw it as an opportunity to unload everything I'd been thinking and feeling. But over time, I realized he wanted the condensed version. For the Expressive that I am, that was a tall order, but I realized I would be encouraging him to listen to me the next time. I also watched his body language so I would know when he'd had enough."

Yvonne has given us our first guidelines:

Know when to stop. Limit sharing to one issue, then invite your mate to talk to you about that issue.

Look for peak talking times. Be sensitive to your

mate's best time of day for talking.

When Keith came home from a business trip, Rhonda looked forward to catching up immediately with all the family news and having Keith give quality attention to the children. Keith, meanwhile, wanted to be greeted by a quiet and uncluttered house. Misunderstandings usually resulted.

Now that they've communicated their needs, Rhonda asks Keith for a quick kiss and "I love you," and then lets him alone to go through the waiting mail. Once he's had time to relax, he comes back out to the family to wrestle with the kids and talk at length with Rhonda. They've learned how to work within the boundaries of realistic expectations.

Write letters and notes. When Danny and Terrie were learning to share their feelings with each other, Danny felt too intimidated to express himself when faced with a conflict. His mind went blank. Instead, going to work and writing Terrie a letter worked for him. Terrie says, "The first time Danny wrote me a letter expressing his feelings, it was painfully honest. But I cherish that letter because it represents my husband's desire to share his heart with me."

Ask questions that can't be answered with one word. Ask questions that take more explanations:

"What was the greatest time you ever had when you were growing up?"

"What funny thing happened at work today?"

"What was the saddest thing that has ever happened to you?"

"How do you feel when our child tells you he/she loves you?"

"Describe your excited feeling by using a color."

"Is there another time you've felt like that?"

Understand that feelings are neither right nor wrong. The initial first flash of an emotion is neither right nor wrong because you didn't choose for it to be there. Although our feelings are influenced by our thinking, we aren't responsible for them until they've surfaced. Then we can make a choice—and that resulting action or attitude is something we *are* responsible for.

For instance, if someone came up to you and hit you in the face, you would most likely immediately feel angry or emotionally hurt. You didn't "decide" to feel that way; it just came out. Those unpleasant feelings of hurt and anger are neither right nor wrong, but your response after being hit can be. If you hit back, that is wrong (unless you're being mugged). If you instead exclaim, "Why did you do that?" or "Stop that!" that's a correct response.

We must be careful, though, because some people identify their opinions as "feelings" and then say it's okay for them to express them. True "feeling words" stem from emotion. We cannot say, "I feel that you are clumsy." We're not expressing a feeling; we're actually stating an opinion—which could be correct or incorrect.

When your spouse shares a true feeling, even if it's unpleasant or you find that feeling inappropriate, he or she has the right to express it. Please don't tell your mate she "can't" feel that way.

At a couples' retreat, a man shared with me how he told his wife she shouldn't feel embarrassed when one of their checks bounced, because it was the bank's fault it happened. I helped him to see that he was rejecting her feeling—which was very real to her—even though he didn't think the situation justified her embarrassment.

Don't try to "fix" the feeling once it's expressed. If your mate says, "That made me feel sad," you may feel compelled to "fix it," making him or her feel better. But by saying, "Oh, just cheer up, you'll feel better," or, "Well, why don't you just tell them that hurt you," you've belittled his or her feelings and most likely diminished the opportunity of his or her sharing again.

Instead of "fixing" feelings, reflect them back. Say things like, "That must have really made you excited. What happened next?" or "I can really hear the sadness in your voice. Do you remember feeling like this any other time?"

Sally and her husband, Jonathan, recently went on a weekend getaway and enjoyed each other's company immensely. As they drove back to their home on Sunday, Jonathan looked over at her with love in his eyes and said, "Honey, this is the closest I think I've ever felt to you."

Sally almost gasped in dismay and thought, *What about all our other close times? Didn't they mean anything to you?* She swallowed her words and tried to smile back at him. Later, as she thought about it, she realized she'd received his comment as a put-down, when he was actually expressing his warm feelings. She was relieved, knowing she hadn't tried to "correct" or "fix" his feeling.

Ask about your spouse's interests. Some men do give feedback about their interests, but because a woman doesn't consider them important, she discounts the importance of his sharing. If she can recognize that listening to his feelings about what's important to him may open him up more, she'll be more encouraged to listen. It's also all right to gently provide possible feeling words.

Give eye contact and undivided attention. As difficult as it may be to put down the carrot you're peeling or turn from the book you're reading, husbands and wives need to communicate that they're totally interested in what their mate has to say. We may not be able to give undivided attention every time our mate talks to us, but we should try to do it as much as possible—especially when he is saying something important to him.

Accept his style of expressing feelings. Amiable Hank and Expressive Shannon discovered they expressed their feelings differently after the death of their child, Chloe. Chloe was one in a set of triplets born to them four years earlier. Though all three survived a difficult birth, Chloe died a month later.

"I felt at peace," Hank says. "I did everything I could while she lived and prayed hard for wisdom from the Lord. Once it was over, there was nothing more I could do. So I wanted to get the cemetery marker right away. Whatever feelings I had, I'd expressed."

Shannon replies, "I thought of Chloe every day. I remembered the important dates, like the times she had surgery or a major crisis happened. Hank didn't want to talk about her, but I wanted to talk about her all the time. At first I interpreted that as meaning he wanted to forget about her. It wasn't until later I realized he just didn't want to review the pain."

"Shannon and I also differed in that I didn't want to know the results of the autopsy report. I didn't want to know if there was something that could have been fixed. Shannon did. I'd decided I'd done all I could, and I didn't want to find out I'd failed. At the viewing, Shannon went in to see Chloe, but I couldn't."

Shannon remembers, "On the second anniversary of Chloe's death, we were at our church's family camp. I got angry at Hank because I thought he knew the meaning of the date and was intentionally ignoring it. I was depressed and Hank asked why. Then I knew he didn't remember the significance of that day. Over time, I've accepted that Hank grieves in a different way than I do and that's okay. My Expressive nature wants to talk about it, but Hank's Amiable temperament wants to lay it aside and rediscover peace."

Be grateful for whatever level of sharing you receive. If all your husband or wife can do is say, "On a scale of 1 to 10, with 10 being intense, I feel 7 about that," accept it. Rejoice in it. You'll be gently and subtly encouraging further deeper sharing by showing your gratitude.

Tell your mate the benefits of sharing with you. Explain gently why it's important to you that he spend time sharing his heart with you. Tell why it makes you feel important and significant and that, in turn, makes you want to meet his needs. Similarly, when he doesn't share with you, you feel less motivated to meet his needs.

Find out what is important to your mate and specifically say that his talking to you about feelings, thoughts, goals, or desires motivates you to please him. And then when he "performs" to the slightest degree, show him you're a person who keeps your word. Please him with his particular "definition of love."

As each of us learns the importance of sharing our God-created emotional dimensions, we'll grow more deeply in love with our mates. We are so thankful that God led us to that first couples' retreat where we learned the importance of communicating our feelings. We believe God can lead you and your mate into further sharing of your feelings. May you be able to trust him for that as well.

Chapter 10

Drifting toward Disillusionment

I looked forward to eating the shrimp salad I was making. My grandmother had taught me her recipe, but just the right amount of red wine vinegar and mayonnaise were needed to give it its tangy, tasty appeal. Before marriage, my father gave each of my creations a taste test. It made me feel important when my father would take a bite and then declare whether it was perfect or needed just a hint more of some seasoning.

I offered a bite to Larry, my husband of one week, for his first taste test. What my father had done for me, I now envisioned my husband continuing.

"Honey, I'm fixing shrimp salad for dinner. You remember, the one that my grandmother fixes. Would you please taste this and tell me whether it needs a little more vinegar or not?"

Larry's eyes didn't even leave the television screen. "Kathy, I don't want to taste it now. I'm sure it will be fine. I'll eat it at dinner."

Doesn't he care about my salad? I wondered, as my tradition lay shattered on the floor. In my mind I knew it wasn't any big deal. But my heart felt like a knife had pricked it—the knife of disillusionment. I never thought it would happen to me, and here I was, feeling it after only one week.

I really didn't intend to hurt Kathy's feelings. I had no idea I was supposed to continue the "taste testing" tradition. If she had explained it to me, I might have had a different attitude, but this wasn't to be the first tradition, expectation, or desire that would go unfulfilled.

We were surprised to see disillusionment enter our marriage so quickly. Yet we shouldn't have been. "No couple who marries is compatible," Christian psychologist H. Norman Wright explains. "This is the shocking statement I share with every couple in the first session of premarital counseling. When they recover from the shock, they're ready to hear the rest. I suggest that it will take the first five to ten years to learn to be compatible. And this means each person will need to change and learn to complement his or her partner." If a husband and wife do not comprehend this truth, their marriage will be more vulnerable to disillusionment.

In reality, every marriage journeys through a cycle of love that includes romance, disillusionment, and joy. These three stages occur again and again. Often, when we're in the disillusionment phase, we wonder whether we've fallen out of love. We may conclude that we've married the wrong person, or that we misinterpreted God's guidance and disobeyed him by marrying this person who is now making us so unhappy.

Society gives us the impression that since we've "fallen out of love," or since this person is not meeting our needs any longer, we have the right to divorce and seek another who *will* be all we need. But God's idea for marriage is a forever kind of commitment that travels through the three stages over and over again, each time learning to make a decision to love. In so doing, we become stronger in our faith, dependence on God, and godly character.

Before we can reach that sort of "marital maturity," however, we need to come to grips with some of the issues that feed disillusionment and discouragement.

The 50-50 Mindset

As we were growing up, the prevailing wisdom about marriage stated that "each person should give 50-50 to the marriage." It sounded reasonable, yet we didn't realize how it contributed to our cycling into disillusionment.

 Kathy and I began slipping into that phase when we noticed the other was no longer giving a full 50 percent. Feeling miffed, we each withdrew from giving to the other, thinking that would get his attention and influence him to fulfill "his" part. Little by little, deeper disillusionment crept in.

 The 50-50 mindset believes the myth that "he who gives more than the other person loses." But God's mindset for couples is: "Love 100 percent, even when he or she isn't lovable, and don't keep score."

We can live out this expectation by not holding back the good things we would do for our mate if she or he were fulfilling our expectations. Every couple should beware of the mentality described by Ed Young when he writes in *Romancing the Home:*

> I witnessed a television wedding recently that was "standard issue" in every way but one.
>
> The bride and groom were formally dressed. There were flowers, beautiful music, and family and friends in attendance. Rings were exchanged; vows were spoken, but with one slight variation. The bride and groom promised to "love and cherish, honor and sustain," but not as long as they both shall live. Oh no. These two promised to keep their vows as long as they both "shall love." Just one letter changes, but oh, what a difference that one letter makes.

Finances and Temperaments

Expressive Mary loves to spend. Her flamboyant temperament and outlook on life require the latest clothing styles and major redecorating projects for her home. And because of her love for people, she impulsively buys gifts for others, thinking, "Sheila will just love this!"

Driver Fred loves money for the sense of power it gives him. It's his ticket to success and status. Therefore, anything prohibiting the accumulation of money is a threat that creates a sense of insignificance.

Analytical Judi finds money to be a faithful friend that brings security. She would rather have a fat balance on her statement than spend it on things she needs.

Amiable John doesn't usually concern himself with money. A hard worker, he usually gets someone else to balance his checkbook and even buy his gifts for him.

If a conflict arises about money, he'd just as soon let the other person have her way.

These general descriptions of the temperaments in relation to money show how opposing temperaments can bring disillusionment into a marriage. Money-related issues are often seen as a reason couples split up, but many financial counselors say those issues are only a symptom of deeper relational problems.

In the past, when I had a second career as a Certified Financial Planner, I advised couples to individually write down every financial goal they could think of and list them by importance. When the husband and wife compared their lists, they could then develop a third list of "our goals." I also advised them to determine a budget.

Once a budget has been established (or even if it hasn't), the question becomes, "Who should pay the bills?" Authors and speakers Yvonne and Bob Turnbull had to work through this conflict. Yvonne says, "I remember a time when Bob turned all the financial responsibility over to me. It seemed sensible since I have a bookkeeping background. I felt intuitively uncomfortable with the arrangement, but thought it would be okay. As time went along, I felt stressed out. I kept telling Bob, 'Make more money. We're not paying our bills.' It became a conflict between us. I was sounding more and more like a nagging wife. Finally, I told him I couldn't handle it anymore. He needed to take leadership by paying the bills."

Bob says, "When Yvonne came to me, I realized I had not given her the protection and leadership she needed. Finances were erecting a wall between us. I hadn't meant to push the burden on her, but I was busy with other things and thought she was doing a good job. Once she shared how she felt, we came to a compromise. I would shoulder the responsibility of making the decisions of which bills would be paid until we got back on our feet, and she would write out the bills and do the paperwork. We began working as a team."

Neither husband nor wife should be individually and exclusively responsible for making all the financial decisions. Doing the paperwork itself doesn't determine leadership. So often, a woman tells us she wants her husband to write out the bills so that he'll be the leader. We tell her it's not paying the bills that's important, but that he's taking leadership in being involved.

Kathy and I usually sit down together at bill paying time and write out the bills together, making any needed decisions as we go along. You may desire that kind of arrangement, but your husband or wife may not want to participate. This is most often true of the Amiable or the Expressive. The Amiable often doesn't have strong feelings about how the money should be spent, and the Expressive doesn't want to work with details. If this is your situation, try to get your spouse involved little by little. The first time you might ask him one question about a decision that needs to be made. The next time you might ask him to help you write out checks. And so on, without overwhelming your spouse with too much information, until he is sharing in this important sphere of marriage.

Credit cards are often an area of conflict within a marriage. Try to wait at least twenty-four hours before charging something you want. After using a credit card, write the amount into the checkbook.

For husbands or wives who tend to overspend, an envelope system can be the solution. On each payday, put cash in envelopes labeled for groceries, entertainment, and other areas. When the money in an envelope is gone, stop spending in that area. When you pay cash, you think more about what you're spending.

Although we cannot force an overspending spouse to put these principles into action, we can use them ourselves and be an example. Sometimes it takes consequences from failure to help someone really make changes. We can trust God to use those consequences to develop maturity within our spouse.

When the Past Is Not Really Over

None of us enter marriage wiped clean from our pasts, yet we rarely acknowledge the influence our pasts have over us.

Margie says, "The biggest illusion I've faced is not realizing the effects my dysfunctional family had on me. With my marriage, I thought I would have a fresh start. The past was behind me, like a closed door. It took six years before I comprehended the huge impact my father's alcoholism brought into my marriage. Then I started working on those issues through counseling and through forcing my dad to deal with his alcoholism."

Here are some other examples of husbands and wives whose pasts influence them now. Let's begin with Paul:

"I have no concept of loyalty," he says. "Therefore, I'm always expecting Anna to leave me because I don't deserve her love. I can see now how my past caused this. In my family, once someone dies, they are never mentioned again. My mother was sick in the hospital and three days after she died, my father pulled me out of a high school class, told me she had died, and sent me back to class. We never mentioned her again."

His wife, Anna, says, "Because both my parents died during my teenage years, I have deep abandonment issues. If Paul is late from work for more than an hour, I feel hysterical. I don't want him to leave me like my parents did."

"When Anna would delay getting home, I felt abandoned," Paul admits. "When I was growing up, I was expected by my father to be home to take care of my brothers. I was held responsible for the choices they made. That expectation of being on time and being responsible made me think Anna didn't love me if she didn't arrive on time."

Paul and Anna have totally different ideas of how they should be treated when they're ill, based upon their childhoods. Expressive Anna says, "I want lots of attention when I'm sick. If Paul will sit down beside me and talk to me, I feel so much better. That's what my mother did for me when I was sick." But Analytical Paul had a different experience. "When I was sick as a child, I was left alone in my room and I enjoyed the quiet. Now I don't want anyone to bother me."

These examples show how unmet expectations can easily create disillusionment. Recognizing their strong influence can help us deal with our disillusionment and make loving choices.

I met Laurie at a women's retreat where I was speaking. She told me how angry she was about her husband's insensitivity to their two daughters. He wouldn't watch any of their soccer games. When I asked her about her childhood, she shared several things and then said, "When I was a high school cheerleader, my father didn't watch me at any of the sports events."

When I pointed out the similarity between the choices of her husband and her father, tears welled into her eyes. "I'm displacing my anger from my father onto Bart, aren't I?"

I agreed. Then we prayed, and Laurie was able to forgive both her father and her husband for not meeting her expectations and creating disillusionment in her marriage.

Are there experiences from your past that are negatively influencing your marriage now? If there are deep issues, you may want to seek professional counseling.

 Over the years I've recognized how my past contributed to my sense of marital disillusionment. My parents' relationship was the epitome of a secure marriage as I grew up. But, shortly after my wedding, my dad suddenly became uninterested in his marriage—none of us ever knew why. In time my parents reconciled, but I was left with an insecure feeling. I already felt I didn't deserve such a wonderful man as Larry. Would he suddenly "wake up" to realize he didn't want to be married, like my dad had done? Those thoughts deepened my doubt about Larry's love. So whenever he seemed distant, I was afraid; and out of my fear grew anger and hurt, which only pushed him further away.

 My childhood also influenced the way I reacted in my marriage. As an only child, I never had to learn to share with a brother or sister. Although I did learn sharing skills through interaction with friends, I received all the attention and love in my home. That may have contributed to my rigidity early in our marriage. In a sense, I had to learn to "share" with Kathy by giving up an expectation that my needs would always be met, sometimes to the exclusion of hers.

The Children Factor

We have had some of our most heated disagreements over issues related to our children—specifically, how to discipline them. As a Driver, I think being strict will whip them into shape. Kathy, an Analytical with a mother's heart, wants to encourage them and be understanding of their mistakes and faults. During the years when Darcy and Mark were in their early teens, this conflict was strongest of all. The more tender Kathy was, the more I perceived it as permissiveness and the stricter I became. The stricter I became, the more tender Kathy became to make up for my "harshness."

One evening, as we lay in bed, we began to again assail each other about the wrong choices the other was making. We both believed strongly we were right. Then, like a lightning bolt, we realized, "We're both wrong! We've each swung the pendulum completely out of balance, and we're each reacting to the other. It's got to stop!"

I agreed to be more understanding and tenderhearted toward Darcy and Mark. Kathy committed to greater consistency in disciplining and holding the children accountable for the rules of our home.

You may think your husband or wife isn't being the parent you want her or him to be. Instead of trying to make your spouse your clone, value and learn from his or her approach to parenting. Remember, "different" isn't necessarily "wrong." Your children need both your and your spouse's input in their lives. If they had two of *you,* one of you wouldn't be needed, and they would be missing out on another way of viewing life. Remember what we said a while back about how spouses "rub off" on each other? It happens the same way in childrearing. Your mate's style influences you, and vice versa, and eventually you achieve a healthy balance.

Discipline isn't the only problem area that arises with children. Children eat up our time and make continual demands. The wise husband and wife carve out time for togetherness, knowing that the best way to love their child is by loving one another and making their own relationship a priority. It's essential that a wife not become so consumed by her children's needs that she neglects time with her husband. She can find a baby-sitter and pay attention to the needs of her husband. Similarly, a husband can take the initiative and plan a time away from the children for him and his wife.

Generally speaking, your children will be an active part of your family for less than half of your marriage. Take steps now to avoid having that marriage partner be a stranger to you when the baby birds leave you an empty nest.

Moving into Joy

Yes, there will be disillusionment in our marriage relationships. But the good news is we can move out of disillusionment and into joy. Here's how.

Take responsibility for your own happiness. Sonia

says, "Before I knew about the cycles of romance, disillusionment, and joy, I thought there was something wrong with me. The disillusionment created even more disillusionment within me because I considered it permanent. Now, I ask myself what I am going to do to get out of it. I can be happy regardless, because of the Lord."

Only God can meet all our needs. When we release our husband or wife from the unrealistic expectation that he or she is responsible for our security or significance, we've taken the first step to moving out of disillusionment.

Choose to love.

During one particular day of disillusionment when Larry was gone flying again, the Lord whispered in my heart, "Tell Larry you love him."

"I will not, Lord. I won't be a hypocrite. I hate him."

"Kathy, I want you to tell Larry you love him."

"But God, if I tell him that, he'll think I'm approving of everything he's doing wrong. No!"

"Then, Kathy," the Lord whispered again, "I want you to *think* it the next time you see Larry."

"Okay. I guess I can think it . . . even if it's not true."

That evening, when I heard Larry come home, my heart beat faster as I told myself I must obey the Lord. I had to think those three little words I had not said or thought for over two years: "I love you."

Larry stepped through the door, I looked him straight in the eye, and I thought, feeling disgruntled and reluctant, *I love you.* Seconds later I mentally added, *But I don't really.*

God used my choice that day to help me see that I

could choose to love Larry even though the feelings weren't there. Over time, as I continued to make that choice, my feelings of love actually returned.

Today, I can look back and see the importance of that step. I found out that choosing to love doesn't mean I approve of everything a person is doing. Winkie Pratney defines love as "a choice for a person's highest good." Within that definition, there is room for disapproving of a mate's behavior. Even though I didn't think I truly loved Larry, God used my decision as a springboard for the healing of our marriage.

 I didn't realize Kathy had made that choice. But it became apparent something was going on. She was no longer a clinging, bitter person. She started expressing gratitude for the things I did and actually became pleasant to be near. I wasn't sure what had happened, but the change was obvious. As Kathy became less needy, she started looking more attractive to me. Her behavior now reminded me of the romantic times of our relationship.

At first nothing really changed in my behavior. I was still spending too much time building a career or trying to relax and recover from my frenetic efforts building that career. But as time progressed and Kathy became more content and confident, I found myself wanting to be at home more. I became less defensive. I listened to Kathy more, and I finally agreed to attend a marriage retreat. She was so much easier to live with that I now found it difficult to dismiss her. Her demands had become requests. Conflicts between us had become discussions. Her previous anger was replaced by contentment. As I look back, I now see how her choices softened my heart, preparing me for the changes God desired for my life.

Author Josh McDowell says that true love causes creative changes in the one loved. This is so true. God created that change within me through Kathy's loving, selfless choices.

In *Joy That Lasts,* Gary Smalley shares a similar change that happened in his marriage as his wife, Norma, "stopped expecting life from me and started looking to God. She realized I not only would not, but could not, fill her life, so she went to the source of life and asked him to fill her." As a result, Norma "realized she wasn't fighting me; she was fighting God's plan for fulfillment." Dr. Neil Anderson puts it this way: "When you seek to play the role of the Holy Spirit in another person's life, you will misdirect that person's battle with God onto yourself." After all, which do you think is more effective at influencing your spouse: your attempts to manipulate, control, and nag; or the continual work of the Holy Spirit?

Reject the possibility of divorce. Unless you're dealing with a mate who is unfaithful (the biblical grounds for divorce), or is physically, sexually, or emotionally abusive (which are reasons for separation), divorce must no longer be an option.

Carol didn't realize that considering the option of divorce was the very thing preventing her marriage from growing. Her husband, Carl, said hurtful things like "You've changed from when we were first married. We don't have anything in common anymore because you've become a Christian." Carol would then reason, "No problem. When the kids are grown, I'll leave him. I can take care of myself." The escape door of a future divorce protected her emotionally from the pain of rejection.

But one day, as Carol and her prayer partner, Kimberly, were praying, Carol told her about this open door labeled "Divorce." Kimberly felt led by the Lord to encourage Carol to close the door, to give up the option of divorce, then thank God for her husband.

"Kimberly, I can't! It'll hurt too much. That door is the only protection I have."

Kimberly replied, "You can make a choice to do it with Jesus' help."

Immediately, Carol envisioned herself hiding behind Jesus. The battle became Jesus' and not hers. She closed the door and gave up divorce as an option. Peace flooded her heart as she committed herself to her marriage regardless of the possible emotional pain. Carol was then able to respond to Carl's kindness with more love. She realized that his efforts at loving her had been there all along. But because she hadn't been committed to their relationship, she was blind to them and focused only on his hurtful reactions.

Now, several years later, Carol says, "I can see that the option of divorce had prevented my vulnerability. When we're vulnerable, we're open to having God reveal our own trouble spots and working on them through our spouse. Without commitment, I didn't grow and my marriage couldn't grow. Carl and I have a growing marriage now. He still has fits of anger, but he's working on them. I have changed too." Carl and Carol have learned what it means to commit to their marriage.

Choose to forgive. Forgiveness can move us from disillusionment into joy as we let the person who wronged us get off the hook labeled "punishment." Punishment wants the person to hurt the way we've been hurt; forgiveness gives them permission to be spared hurt.

Forgiveness is a choice before it ever becomes a good feeling. We must first forgive with our will, even as our feelings strongly object. Our loving feelings may or may not follow. Then when Satan reminds us of that person's failings, we can confidently remind him we have forgiven the person.

It's important to note that forgiveness is not the same thing as trust. When our mate is unfaithful, we can forgive him or her and seek reconciliation, even if he or she is not repentant. Forgiveness is primarily for *our* benefit, not our mate's. But trust is something that must be rebuilt, something that develops and grows as our spouse shows evidence of faithfulness and commitment to the marriage.

Focus on the positive in your mate. Even if you're married to the most wonderful person alive, you can still experience dissatisfaction in your marriage if you focus only on his annoying habits or actions. No spouse is perfect. Whether you're in a period of romance, disillusionment, or joy in your marriage has a lot to do with whether you are focusing on the positives or negatives.

Focus on the good times and fond memories you've experienced. What are the qualities that attracted you to your mate in the first place? Chances are those qualities haven't changed, but your perception of them may have. Can you again regard them as the strengths you first saw?

If needed, seek professional Christian counseling.

Some problems are beyond our ability to work alone, and therapy may be needed. Even if your spouse won't attend sessions with you, it still will be beneficial for you to talk with a counselor to gain an objective perspective.

God can work an instantaneous deliverance from disillusionment in your marriage. Or he may choose to take you both through a process of growth by reading a book together, going on a marriage enrichment retreat, talking your problems over with some trusted friends, or seeking professional Christian counseling. In whatever way he leads you, trust him to empower you to make loving choices in your marriage.

Benefits of Choosing to Love

As we travel through the cycle and move out of disillusionment by choosing love, we'll reap the benefits outlined in 2 Peter 1:5-8:

> Now for this very reason also, applying all diligence, in your faith supply moral excellence, and in your moral excellence, knowledge; and in your knowledge, self-control, and in your self-control, perseverance, and in your perseverance, godliness; and in your godliness, brotherly kindness, and in your brotherly kindness, love. For if these qualities are yours and are increasing, they render you neither useless nor unfruitful in the true knowledge of our Lord Jesus Christ (NASB).

In other words, by being diligent, you'll experience the fruits of:

ellence: you'll resist temptations of

e: you'll know how to minister to others

- Self-control: you'll be able to control your emotional life better

- Perseverance: it won't be as difficult for you to continue making godly choices

- Godliness: you'll grow closer to being who God wants you to be

- Kindness: you'll be able to make kind choices for the good of others, especially your spouse

- Love: the ultimate fruit will be an ability to unconditionally love even when your mate is unlovely.

If we choose divorce rather than unconditional love and acceptance, we will miss out on this growth potential. Let us clarify, though, that if you are being abused, God does not want you to persevere in that situation. There are limits to the ungodliness he wants you to suffer. But if you are not in an abusive situation, yet your husband or wife does not cooperate with your plans for a great marriage, we say with confidence: look to God to meet your needs. He can give you the strength to accept and love your spouse.

Making a choice to love in order to climb out of disillusionment won't be easy, but it can bring incalculable rewards. Consider Tom Anderson's story:

I made a vow to myself on the drive down to the vacation beach cottage to be with Evelyn. For two weeks I would try to be a loving husband and father. Totally loving. No ifs, ands, or buts.

After the long drive, I wanted to sit and read. Evelyn suggested a walk on the beach. I started to refuse, but then I thought, *Evelyn's been alone here with the kids all week and now she wants to be alone with me.* We walked on the beach while the children flew their kites.

So it went. Two weeks of not calling the Wall Street investment firm where I am a director. A visit to the shell museum, though I usually hate museums. (And I enjoyed it.) Holding my tongue while Evelyn's getting ready made us late for a dinner date. Relaxed and happy, that's how the whole vacation passed. I made a new vow to keep on remembering to choose love.

There was one thing that went wrong with my experiment, however. On the last night at our cottage, preparing for bed, Evelyn stared at me with the saddest expression.

"What's the matter?" I asked her.

"Tom," she said, in a voice filled with distress, "do you know something I don't?"

"What do you mean?"

"Well . . . that checkup I had several weeks ago . . . Tom, you've been so good to me. Am I dying?"

It took a moment for it all to sink in. Then I burst out laughing. "No, honey," I said, wrapping her in my arms. "You're not dying; I'm just starting to live!"

How would your spouse react if you committed to love as Tom Anderson did? Would she think only her upcoming death would make you change? Don't wait for a crisis. Choose now to put God's brand of love into action: choose an unconditional love that will move you out of disillusionment into joy.

Chapter 11

But I Don't Feel Sexy

I slammed the telephone down, muttering, "He did it again." I had just talked with Larry and he was working overtime again. Again! *He makes me so mad.*

Suddenly, scenes from our lovemaking session the previous night flitted through my mind. All morning, I'd been basking in those sensual feelings, but now I felt a chill.

"Why did he spoil it? He better not expect a repeat tonight, that's for sure."

As I complained about my discontent, questions rumbled through my mind. "Why is it so hard for me to have an orgasm? Why do I feel so sexy sometimes and other times it's of least importance? How is Larry able to disregard my unhappiness and want sex anyway? Why do I still feel embarrassed about sex, as if God is hiding his eyes? Oh, Lord, why do all these things bother me so much? Help me!"

I was truly puzzled by Kathy's hot and cold responses to our lovemaking. Why did everything have to be perfect before she could fully respond or even be interested? Why couldn't she set aside her concerns and worries like I did and enjoy my attention? After all, I sure had a high interest in sex, and it clearly was the number one way I wanted to demonstrate my love for her. It bothered me that her interest seemed so inconsistent.

As our relationship weakened, my interest in sex seemed less acute, and I poured myself into my career and hobbies. At least they gave me a sense of satisfaction, while Kathy seemed rarely satisfied.

 We aren't the only ones who have struggled in the area of sex in our marriage. Can you relate to any of these situations?

Chelsea, an Expressive, soaks in a bubble bath after a long day of caring for the children. Her momentary bliss is broken by a pair of her panties flying across the bathroom. Todd, her Driver husband, tossed them to demonstrate his interest in lovemaking. Instead of sparking sexual desire, anger flashes through her entire body.

Thomas, an Amiable, has such a strong desire to satisfy his wife, Ginny, that he won't initiate lovemaking unless he expects a good result before taking a risk.

Frank, an Analytical, takes his Amiable wife Lydia's reluctance at lovemaking as personal rejection. Lydia struggles with anger at times when she feels used.

Truly, the sexual relationship is often misunderstood and mishandled. How do you and your spouse consider your sexual relationship? Here's an exercise* developed by Charles M. Sell, author of *Achieving the Impossible: Intimate Marriage*. Each spouse should read through each statement and rate his or her reaction on a scale of 1 to 5 (1=Agree strongly; 5=Disagree strongly).

*Used by kind permission.

- Every couple should have, and read, a good sex manual.

- I respect sex because of its role in producing children.

- A couple can learn to become more interested in sex.

- A woman's menstrual cycle affects her interest in sexual experiences.

- A woman's orgasm always depends on her husband's ability to produce it.

- A wife may not always have to have an orgasm every time she has intercourse.

- One of the strong messages of sexual intercourse is that it says you are wanted and needed.

- Sex is for oneness, and oneness really makes sex worthwhile.

- A couple should take entire evenings and weekends to share together sensually and to develop their sex life.

- I feel somewhat guilty about having sex in marriage.

- If a woman never has an orgasm, the couple should seek counseling.

y like it when you say things that make
ike a man (or a woman).

ice is one of the things women want most in
sensual experience.

- Physical variety and intensity is what most men want in their sexual experience.

- Variation in positions is a good way to improve a sexual relationship.

- It is acceptable for a man to desire and enjoy oral sex with his wife.

- It is acceptable for a woman to desire and enjoy oral sex with her husband.

- Sexual intercourse should be abstained from during the wife's menstrual period.

- In order for Christians to cultivate their relationship in marriage, they should try to totally abandon themselves to each other in their sexual expression.

The goal of this exercise is to hear your mate's opinions and share your own. Although we may all agree God is the creator of our sexual desires, the ways we use that gift are often open to discussion. Most wives think their husbands have the attitude expressed by Josh McDowell: "When's the best time to have sex? Any days that start with the letter T: Tuesdays, Thursdays, Tundays, Taturdays, and Today and Tomorrow."

Three Kinds of Sexual Response

Not only do women and men view sex differently, they respond differently within lovemaking. None of these responses are more desirable than the others; they are just different.

These responses can be broken down into three categories: erotic, intimate, and recreational. These reactions describe how a man or woman might feel during or at the conclusion of a sexual encounter. Difficulties arise when only one reaction is considered valuable or if a spouse is disappointed that her mate doesn't experience the same feelings she does.

Denny says, "I feel threatened when I'm feeling intimate and Patricia said she had fun. I recently heard a radio psychologist say there are some people who only feel love in a sexual context. I really identified with that. I feel loved when Pat and I are sexual. If I ask her if she felt intimate like I did, and she says she had fun, then I don't feel loved."

Denny is learning that Patricia can experience something different during lovemaking and still have received his love and loved him in return.

Sexual Myths, Sexual Truths

Myths about sex and sexuality abound. Here are a few of the most common—and problematic—misconceptions couples can struggle with.

1. *If I'm not always wanting sex, I must not be a very sensual person.*
    The truth is we all vary in our sexual desires, and there

is a wide sway within what is "normal." This is particularly true when dealing with male/female differences. Studies indicate that a woman's libido rises and falls according to her twenty-eight-day ovulation cycle. A man can have sexual thoughts every few minutes.

One expert in the field of sexual counseling gives this guideline: if you're under forty-five and desire sex less than once every two weeks, or over forty-five and desire sex less than once a month, he advises counseling.

2. Sex is the only way to experience feelings.

Since most men don't easily acknowledge their feelings, sex becomes a way of demonstrating emotion. For instance, if a man loses his job, his wife may be surprised when he wants to make love that evening. But that was the closest he could come to allowing himself to feel his buried emotions.

3. Only spontaneous sex is true sex.

"Early in our marriage, Carl and I would cuddle by our fireplace, reading or playing cards," says Julie. "We frequently made great love on the floor. It was spontaneous and fun. Now, with the arrival of our twins, spontaneity is the farthest thing from our minds. Since we almost have to schedule sexual time into our planners, I'm really disillusioned. It just doesn't seem like real sex."

Carl and Julie are finding out the truth: sex must be planned. It may not seem as fun when we have to write it into our schedule, but if we don't, we may not experience as much closeness in our busy lives.

4. Sex comes naturally.

Although God has given us a natural desire to become

one with that beloved husband or wife, he didn't necessarily give us an inborn knowledge of how to sexually please another person. No wonder the bride and groom are stressed out on their wedding night. The couple who have restrained from sex before marriage may expect God to bless them with a wonderful sexual experience from their first night together. They may be shocked or surprised when things don't go quite as planned.

Sex is a learned skill; therefore we may not experience a blissful beginning even if we've obeyed God's command. We are to follow his rules, not because we'll have good sex, but because his rules are best for us. Besides, this is definitely an area where practice is fun!

5. I can put our sexual relationship on hold while we're busy with other things and rejuvenate it later.

With the demands of career and family, women in particular can easily think, "Sex can wait until later, when I can give it attention." Such an attitude may contribute to a poor relationship that needs a whole lot more than attention to sex.

6. I should have sex only if I'm in love with my spouse.

Della sat in front of me at the retreat center. She averted her eyes as she whispered, "I don't love my husband anymore. When we have sex, I feel as if I'm a . . . prostitute."

Della incorrectly believed she must feel loving toward her husband in order to have sex with him. For several minutes I tried to help Della see that she was actually making a decision of love that honored God when she responded to her husband's needs. My advice to Della was based on the fact that her husband was not abusive or demeaning. If a husband is using sex as a destructive tool, a wife should not force herself to participate. But withholding sex just because we don't feel those warm, fuzzy emotions is unwise and may even be harmful to the relationship. Professional Christian counseling may be helpful in some cases.

7. *If a sexual technique worked once, it should work all the time.*

Men have a tendency to focus on this myth; it is a very easy trap to fall into. The woman's response is best approached without depending upon a particular method or technique. The creative power of variety is a key to pleasing our wives. Men must learn to view their wife's body like a piano with many keys. Each time they make love, he can play a different melody.

Why We Struggle with Sex

There are many challenges couples face when they try to create a satisfying, God-honoring sexual relationship. These are among the most common.

The lure of fantasy. Fantasy is subtly created with the help of movies, TV, advertisements, and romance novels. From them, we can easily begin to believe:

- Everybody's having sex all the time, with everyone else.

- Adultery is acceptable and can even be a positive influence to brighten a sagging marriage.

- The hero always knows how to love perfectly and fully, even the first time.

- If you've fallen out of love, you should divorce and find someone who can really meet your needs.

- Becoming aroused through Internet chat rooms will increase my sexual satisfaction with my spouse.

Although we will never completely prevent these ideas from bombarding our minds, we can resist them with the truth. God wants us to learn and grow together within the marital bonds of love, being patient and understanding.

The idea that sex is "dirty." Many men, but especially women, grow up with the mistaken idea that sex is wrong and dirty.

In *Romancing the Home,* Ed Young explains, "Sex is a God-given need meant to be satisfied in the highest, holiest, and most satisfying way: in the context of marriage. The idea that sex is wrong or perverted or unappealing is found nowhere in the Bible. Too many, especially women, have been brought up to think that sex is something to be endured rather than enjoyed, and the wife's role is simply to put up with her husband's desire for this unpleasant ritual of marriage. . . . Married love is a part of the excitement and thrill and romance of life's most intimate human bond."

When Darcy and Mark were in their early teens, I asked them about some music they were listening to that I found offensive. I commented with disgust, "But they're singing about sexual intercourse!" Seconds later, I thought, *Maybe they think I meant the act of sex is disgusting. Oh, no, I've ruined my children's concept of sex!*

Several years ago, Larry and I went to bed early, planning to enjoy lots of sexual attention. We locked our bedroom door and had just started when we heard Darcy come home from work and then knock on our door. She wanted something from our room. Larry dressed, got the item and unlocked the door, handing it to her. As she left, she said, "It's sure a good thing you can't have any more children—otherwise I'd have six or seven brothers and sisters."

Larry and I laughed. I was also relieved. God had somehow overridden my inappropriate comment. Our children seem to have a healthy view of sex.

If you wonder whether God closes his eyes in embarrassment when you make love, consider this. The Bible freely talks about sex and encourages its enjoyment. Proverbs 5:18-19 says, "Let your fountain be blessed, and rejoice in the wife of your youth. As a loving hind and a graceful doe, let her breasts satisfy you at all times; be exhilarated always with her love" (NASB).

All of the Bible's Song of Solomon (NASB) refers to sex vividly and with enthusiasm: "May he kiss me with the kisses of his mouth!" (1:2). "Let his left hand be under my head and his right hand embrace me" (2:6). Chapter 4 is the dialogue between Solomon and his new bride on their wedding night. Among other sensual things, the bridegroom says, "Your two breasts are like two fawns, twins of a gazelle" (4:5). Chapter 7 is full of references to parts of the body and how they enjoy them in sexual union.

The apostle Paul instructs us: "Let the husband fulfill his duty to his wife, and likewise also the wife to her husband. The wife does not have authority over her own body, but the husband does; and likewise also the husband does not have authority over his own body, but the wife does. Stop depriving one another, except by agreement for a time that you may devote yourselves to prayer, and come together again lest Satan tempt you because of your lack of self-control" (1 Cor. 7:3-5, NASB).

In all the Bible, marital sexual fulfillment is considered good and sacred. Think of it this way. A woman's clitoris has no purpose other than to provide pleasure. If God had not wanted a woman to enjoy sex, why would he have created an organ that has no other purpose?

Don't make the mistake that Sandie inadvertently made. One evening she walked out of the bathroom after taking her shower. Her husband, Jon, smiled and winked. "Want to make love tonight, honey?" he asked.

"But I just took my shower!" Sandie protested. Jon's face dropped as she had just communicated that sex would make her dirty.

Past abuse. Often, a woman has trouble having a healthy sexual viewpoint because she was sexually abused or molested as a child. This can deeply affect the sexual relationship with her husband. Yet she may not realize the influence it has upon her.

Cliff and Joyce Penner, authors of the book *The Gift of Sex,* say, "For a woman who was so abused, her sexuality has been aroused prematurely, and it has been associated with shame, demand, immobilization, and lack of power. It may also have been the girl's only way to get 'love.'"

Professional help is usually necessary, yet there is hope that such difficulties can be overcome.

Premarital sexual involvement.

This is a problem which we regret followed us into our marriage. Heavy petting and inappropriate touching hung over our dating years, even though we tried again and again to break its bondage over us. Once we were married and had the freedom to engage in this gift from God, we never anticipated its painful influence.

I felt angry toward Larry for not preventing our sin. I reasoned, "Since I couldn't control myself before marriage, I don't deserve to enjoy sex now. Larry shouldn't enjoy it either!" But he did, and that bothered me. He didn't seem to be affected by our premarital sin as much as I did, and I wanted him to suffer like I was.

I was confused and frustrated by Kathy's inconsistent responses during that time. Why can't Kathy just put this behind her? I told her, "Just realize you're forgiven. Stop holding yourself hostage."

I felt threatened as a lover. Why couldn't I satisfy her every time? I tried to remind myself that women don't usually have an orgasm every time, but I was still frustrated. Kathy assured me I was a good lover, and, over time, she improved. That gave me confidence to be patient.

Christian counselor Roger Hillerstrom refers to our experience when he says, "Every couple coming to me for counseling who have had premarital sexual relations have had postmarital sexual adjustment problems. It happens that the sexual arousal of most of us can be conditioned very quickly. When a couple is sexually involved prior to marriage, they are conditioning themselves to respond to it. I have talked with many married couples who have said, 'Before we were married, we had a great sex life! Exciting, fulfilling, and enjoyable. But on our wedding night, for some reason, it died.' What happened on their wedding night? That illicitness that had become a conditioned sexual stimulation was taken away."

For those of us who struggle along these lines, there is hope. I found freedom when I first forgave Larry and then myself. My sin was not greater than any other sin. Just as God longs to forgive any sin, mine qualified for that privilege. I couldn't wipe out the past, but I could give up my bitterness toward myself and Larry.

Remember Chelsea, whose story we shared at the beginning of this chapter, and her anger at Todd? Her response had its roots in their sexual involvement when dating as teens. Only fourteen, Chelsea thought she had to give in to Todd's advances to keep him as a boyfriend. She felt powerless and used. After fourteen years of marriage, this Christian couple is still working their way through a process of forgiveness.

If this is your struggle, forgive yourself and believe God wants to forgive you. He wants you to enjoy the blessings of sex with your husband or wife.

Feeling used. Someone has said, "Women give sex to get love; men give love to get sex." God created men and women with that perspective. Unless that truth is understood, it's easy for women to feel used.

A woman most often feels used when her husband doesn't realize that "sex starts in the kitchen." He may ignore her all day long, but at night, he suddenly wants to pay attention to her. But conversation and affection aren't what he has in mind.

Because a man can compartmentalize his feelings and experiences into a part of his brain and then concentrate on sex, wives may think he's insensitive to their needs. A husband and wife may have just had a fight, and he can put it out of his mind as soon as testosterone reminds him of his sexual needs. It will be difficult for her to understand what he's experiencing, but if she will, it will go a long way to helping her not take his behavior personally.

Regardless, she can calmly express her perspective by saying, "I feel used because I need attention and love expressed during the day. My expectation was that we would build each other up during the day. What was your expectation?" By telling him at times other than a sexual encounter, he may eventually be swayed.

Don't wait for him to initiate hand holding or hugs and kisses. Reach out to him and model for him what you'd like. Express your desires, but do it in a gentle, loving way, without anger. And without withholding sex.

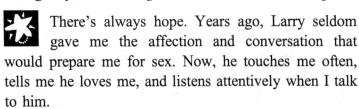 There's always hope. Years ago, Larry seldom gave me the affection and conversation that would prepare me for sex. Now, he touches me often, tells me he loves me, and listens attentively when I talk to him.

Husbands do not intend to diminish their wife's sense of security. And we're often surprised to find out about the hurt we unintentionally inflicted. The Bible tells us to love our wives as Christ loved the church

(Eph. 5:25). We must take the initiative to choose daily to meet our wife's needs for conversation and affection. This is a choice that spiritual leadership demands.

Knowing how important this is to Kathy, I have learned to affirm my love for her daily. Some days I tell her I love her several times. Whenever I walk by Kathy, I'll reach out and tenderly touch her. And if she wants to talk, I give her my complete attention. Initially, I did those things because I knew she enjoyed and wanted it. Now I find myself spontaneously doing it because I enjoy it and know I'm meeting her needs from my heart. Although it's not my motive, I find she's more responsive sexually.

Enjoying God's Gift

Sex, in a way, starts in the brain. Generally speaking, women don't hold sex uppermost in their minds. Men do. But women can choose to *think* about it and thus increase their responsiveness.

 When I wrote a Bible study about the Song of Solomon, entitled "Romantic Love: Your Father's Gift," Larry thought he'd died and gone to heaven. Since I was studying God's view of sex several hours a day, my appetite for it increased dramatically. That showed me the value of choosing to think about it.

We husbands can help our wives think about sex by giving *them* what *they* need—affection, conversation, and attention to *their* interests. (That means fixing the faucet.) It really is to our benefit.

 It also helps to talk about sex. I can remember in our early marriage being embarrassed by Larry's unrestrained talk about sex. I can now speak freely about our sexual relationship. I can tell Larry if something he's doing is uncomfortable or not being effective. Referring to our joy in sex during the day stirs my interest.

If this is uncomfortable for you, try to broach the subject little by little. Try reading the Song of Solomon aloud to each other. Read a chapter from a book about sex and discuss it. Write a letter to your spouse explaining how you feel. Any steps you take will enhance your ability to enjoy your sexual times together.

In fact, there are many excellent books written from a biblical perspective that can help couples understand God's plan for sex and learn about the ways the body functions during sexual arousal.

Take the initiative. Plan a time away for the weekend. Make the choice to touch your spouse in a sexual way when you're alone, communicating your joy about this special gift God has given you.

Few of us arrive at a perfect sexual relationship regardless of how long we're married. But think of it this way: it sure will be fun striving for it. Every bit of effort you put toward that goal will pay dividends. Decide now to grow in your sexual awareness and desire.

Chapter 12

For Better, for Worse, for Real

More than twenty-five years ago, as I walked down that aisle toward my Prince Charming, I had no idea of the challenges and joys awaiting us. I'm sure there are still many more to come. But I'm so grateful we were willing to let God be victorious in our lives and bring us through some very difficult times. It has been worth it.

Recently, at two different women's retreats where I was speaking, two women came up to me to remind me of my contact with them before. As I had counseled them during their churches' retreats, they each shared similar stories with me: their husbands were horrible, insensitive, and unwilling to work on their marriage. They didn't know how they could hold on. I could only give some inadequate advice in view of their great pain, pray with them, and trust that God could make a difference.

Now both women were telling me how great it was to be married to those same husbands who, a year or two earlier, had caused them such pain. The joy on their faces and the light in their eyes were visual proof of the work God had done in restoring the love between husband and wife. Both shared how as a couple they were involved in their churches, even reaching out to help other hurting marriages. "I'm so glad I didn't give up," each woman said. "God is more powerful than I imagined."

Of course, realistically, I know not every marriage has been restored to true joy. But who knows which ones will enjoy a renewed love relationship? I could not have imagined that Larry and I would now share such a fantastic love. He is my best friend, lover, encourager, counselor, and number-one fan. Although we still have disagreements, I experience a tremendous security even during those times of tension.

As we worked through our problems, and my love for Kathy was renewed, I had no idea that the depth of my love for her could grow even more. I am amazed each day at our deepening relationship, and I can honestly say I find myself more in love with her each year. I believe this is what God intended for our marriages: ever-expanding appreciation, growing intimacy, and enhanced love. These are the hallmarks that God would desire each of our marriages to experience. It merely takes unselfish choices.

I pray that those of you who are struggling in your relationship will be filled with hope when you realize restoration can take place. For those of you who have a good relationship, I pray you will be encouraged to explore the great adventure of growing even deeper in your marriage.

 How do you know if your marriage is growing? It is marked by realizing and accepting your spouse's imperfections, understanding your mate's needs for significance and security, and accepting the differences of your spouse and appreciating the benefits those differences bring. It is loving your spouse as God made him or her—for better, for worse, for real.

The greatest building block to a better marriage is . . . a good marriage!

We challenge you to make a fresh commitment to reach for that better marriage. Our prayers are with you as you make loving, unselfish, God-honoring choices.

To reach Kathy and Larry for possible speaking engagements or correspondence, write to them at P.O. Box 1058, Placentia, CA 92871.